Art and Law

The Copyright Debate

Edited by

Morten Rosenmeier & Stina Teilmann

DJØF Publishing
2005

Art and Law: An Introduction
1st edition, 1st issue

Coverdesign: Engel Graphic Design

Typeface used on the bookcover (and the title page):
Kontrapunkt Light

The Kontrapunkt font is designed by the identity firm, Kontrapunkt A/S,which owns all rights to its use, including copyrights. The font may be used freely provided Kontrapunkt appears, and is properly cited, as its designer.

Printed by: Narayana Press, Gylling
Bound by: Damm's Forlagsbogbinderi, Randers

Printed in Denmark 2005
ISBN 87-574-1298-8

Published with support from
Det Finneske Legat
Udvalget til beskyttelse af videnskabeligt arbejde,
Akademikernes Centralorganisation

DJØF Publishing
Lyngbyvej 17
Box 2702
2100 Copenhagen Ø, Denmark
Phone: (0045) 39 13 55 00
Fax: (0045) 39 13 55 55
e-mail: forlag@djoef.dk
www.djoef-forlag.dk

Acknowledgements

The editors wish to thank the following for their financial support:

The Committee for Research Conduct under The Danish Confederation of Professional Associations; The Social Sciences Research Council of Denmark; the Department of Comparative Literature, University of Copenhagen; Det Finneske Legat; the Faculty of Law, University of Copenhagen; and Udvalget til beskyttelse af videnskabeligt arbejde, Akademikernes Centralorganisation.

Sara Koch co-organized the conference, 'Legal Frameworks'; Professor Charles Lock has been an ever-dependable source of practical advice and learned encouragement.

Contents

Art and Law: An Introduction

Stina Teilmann[*]

Over the course of time, the spheres of art and law have never been entirely separate. Early Western civilization saw perhaps the fiercest clash yet when Plato declared poets and artists unwanted in his Republic. Art and literature were to be outlawed because they deal in fiction, what is not the case. In the Republic's hierarchy of truth art had had been placed at the bottom. 'Shadowy images' such as mirror reflections and works of fine art were at a mere third remove from the truth. Plato illustrates this by referring to the nature of 'a bed'. Primarily, the bed exists as a divinely given idea. Second, there are individual beds, manufactured by carpenters. Lastly, there are versions of a bed that a painter can make. As such, art is a second-degree simulation of truth; it imitates appearances, not essences. An artist, at best, is capable of nothing more than deceiving his audience into believing that he is a workman who has made a thing. Because of its dubious relation to the truth, art corrupts the mind of the citizen. Hence Plato's ban.[1]

Since Plato's times the reputation of art has improved. Aristotle endorsed the human instinct for imitation: *mimēsis*. Indeed the *Poetics* has given us to understand that there is nothing sus-

* Ph.D. Author of *British and French Copyright: A Historical Account of Aesthetic Implications* (2004)

1. See the tenth book of 'The Republic.' Plato, 'The Republic', (Oxford: Oxford University Press, 1972).

pect about the fact that art is imitation.[2] Encounters have continued between art and the law. The law has consistently endeavoured to delineate a distinction between legitimate and illegitimate practices of art. Blasphemy, obscenity, forgery, and libel have been rubrics of the law used to carry out such regulation. Meanwhile, art has continued to challenge the significance of the various applied legal frameworks and to transgress the limits of *artistic freedom* as inferred by the law.

When the Western World moved into the 'New Economy' one particular crossing point between art and law became immensely important: intellectual property law, including copyright law. Copyright in artistic works is the topic of this volume. For as one contributor remarks: 'While many fields of law (obscenity law, tax law, environmental law, public funding related laws, etc.) have a bearing on art and aesthetics it is difficult to find other fields (outside copyright law) that would with an equal capacity partake both in the legitimation and deligitimation of artists (legal subjects) and artworks (legal objects) and in the regulation of the normative basis of the art market.'

The law on copyright – unlike most laws regulating art – came into being as a concession to artists. In the eighteenth and nineteenth centuries copyright laws were enacted in most Western countries, securing creators some revenue from their works. Britain was the first country in the world to introduce copyright: the Statute of Anne 1710 was enacted to protect literary works. A century-and-a-half later, the Fine Arts Act 1862 extended copyright protection to artistic works. France took an approach different from the British subject-specific copyright law: the Revolutionary Copyright Act of 1793 granted copyright to artists, authors and composers alike.[3]

2. Aristotle, 'Poetics,' in *Classical Literary Criticism*, ed. D.A. Russell and M. Winterbottom (Oxford: Oxford University Press, 1972), 51-90.
3. The first U.S. copyright act, 'The Original Copyright Act', as it was labelled, of 1790 was basede on the Statute of Anne. In Denmark art was first protected by 'Loven om beskyttelse af Billedkunst 1837'. The first law on authors' rights was 'Forfatterloven' of 29 December 1857. In Norway the Law of 8 November 1876 and in Sweden the Law of 3 May 1867 introduced copyright.

In the beginning, the purpose of copyright law was to protect creators and publishers against unauthorized reprints and engravings. Gradually copyright acquired a much broader scope. In the nineteenth century a work (literary, artistic or musical) grew to be defined as an immaterial entity. Reproduction of the work 'by any means' and 'in any medium' became a violation. Since the early twentieth century, as a result, it has been considered an infringement of copyright to copy a fragment of a work or to produce an adaptation of it without authorization. Today, accordingly, artists are likely to find themselves on either side of the law: as the artist whose work is protected, or as the artist whose work copyright protects against.

The essays in this volume all explore copyright on the threshold between art and law. Most of them take a legal perspective on art; others contribute a perspective on the law from an artistic point of view.

When viewing art through the lens of copyright law, two matters present themselves with some urgency. First, there is the question of rationales for copyright. Theories of copyright present different views of art as an object and a category of copyright. Roman law identified the crux of the matter when it acknowledged the importance of matter:

> When someone makes something for himself [for example a vase of gold] out of another's materials, Nerva and Proculus are of the opinion that the maker owns that thing because what has just been made previously belonged to no one. Sabinus and Cassius, on the other hand, take the view that natural reason requires that the owner of the materials should be the owner of what is made from them, since a thing cannot exist without that of which it is made. [...] There is, however, the intermediate view of those who correctly hold that if the thing can be returned to its original components, the better view is that propounded by Sabinus and Cassius but that if it cannot be so reconstituted, Nerva and Proculus are sounder.[4]

Art is distinct from other major objects of copyright, such as literature and music, in its being vested in a unique material

4. Gaius, second book: 'Everyday issues or Golden words'. Cited from Ditlev Tamm, *Roman Law and European Legal History* (Copenhagen: DJØF Publishing, 1997), p. 91. See also Peter Stein, *Roman Law in European History* (Cambridge: Cambridge University Press, 1999).

form. Unlike literary and musical works, an artwork (even after Andy Warhol) typically exists as a unique original. This uniqueness is just as much of an asset for the creator – possibly of highest value – as is the copyright in the artistic work. Diverse systems of copyright – whether they rely on economic, cultural, personality rights, literary property right or other theories of copyright – provide different ways of tackling this issue in the protection of art.[5]

A further matter of significance raised by the link between copyright and law is the law's effectiveness. Is the law of copyright equipped to protect art in the way intended by legislators? What types of creations are to be included under the legal category of art – and is it appropriate to have such a category? Is the so-called idea/expression dichotomy (which divides a work into a non-copyrightable idea and a copyrightable expression) valid for all types of works? More generally, as some of the contributors here point out, it is essential that the law continues to be assessed to ensure that copyright's protection of art is satisfactory not only to the mechanics of copyright law, but to artists, and the to public as well.

From the viewpoint of art, copyright law is both a major regulator and a powerful cultural sign. Art has never conformed to what has been defined as such by the law of copyright. It exists in a continual process of transformation: art redefines itself incessantly. Recently, copyright law has served as the specific con-

5. On theories of copyright see Francis J. Kase, *Copyright Thought in Continental Europe: Its Development, Legal Theories and Philosophy. A Selected and Annotated Bibliography.* (South Hackensack, NJ: Fred B. Rothman & Co, 1967). On the economic theory of copyright see Richard Watt, *Copyright and Economic Theory. Friends or Foes?* (Cheltenham, UK: Edward Elgar, 2000). On the cultural argument for copyright see Marquis de Condorcet, "Fragments sur la liberté de la presse" (1776), in *Œuvres de Condorcet*, ed. M.-F. Arago (Paris: Didot, 1847), 253-314. On the personality rights theory, see Immanuel Kant, "Von der Unrechtmäßigkeit der Büchernachdrucks", *Berlinische Monatsschrift* 5, no. May (1785): 403-417 and Johann Gottlieb Fichte, "Beweis der Unrechtmässigkeit des Büchernachdrucks. Ein Räsonnement und ein Parabel," *Berlinische Monatsschrift* 21 (1793): 443-483 On the theory of literary property rights see Justin Hughes, "The Philosophy of Intellectual Property", *Georgetown Law Journal* 77, no. 2 (1988): 287-366.

text of certain art projects. Here the artist ceases to be the passive subject, as defined by the law, who awaits his share of the cake, but becomes a reflective counterpart to the law. Art thus can come to serve as a privileged space of critique and analysis of the notion of copyright. For example, severe resistance has been mustered against copyright law's propertization of creativity. Inasmuch as art is not restricted by an obligation to uphold the internal logic and to accept the basic premises of copyright law it can serve as a framework for testing the validity of the cultural and social assumptions of copyright law. Artistic freedom, optimal conditions for creativity and public access to art were fundamental values in the early days of copyright law. It is a nice question whether these values have survived the property orientation of the law.

The contributions to this book were originally presented as papers at a conference entitled 'Legal Frameworks: Intellectual Property and Visual Art', held on 1-2 October, 2002, organised by the Faculty of Law and the Department of Comparative Literature at the University of Copenhagen. Of late, there has been a growing interest in this field. Notably, works such as Laurence Lessig's *Free Culture: How Big Media Uses Technology and the Law to Lock Down Culture and Control Creativity* (2004), Joost Smiers' *Art under Pressure: Promoting Cultural Diversity in the Age of Globalization* (2003), *Dear Images: Art, Copyright and Culture* edited by Daniel McClean and Karsten Schubert (2002), Simon Stokes' *Art and Copyright* (2001) and Paul Kearns' *The Legal Concept of Art* (1998) have all contributed to a vibrant debate on art and copyright.[6]

6. Lavrence Lessig, *Free Culture: How Big Media Uses Technology and the Law to Lock Down Culture and Control Creativity* (London: Penguin, 2004). Joost Smiers, *Art under Pressure: Promoting Cultural Diversity in the Age of Globalization*. (London, New York: Zed Books, 2003); Daniel McClean and Karsten Schubert, eds., *Dear Images: Art, Copyright and Culture* (London: Institute of Contemporary Art and Ridinghouse, 2002); Simon Stokes, Art and Copyright. 2ed. (Oxford: Hart Publishing, 2003 (2001)); Paul Kearns, *The Legal Concept of Art* (Oxford: Hart Publishing, 1998). See also the list of further reading at the end of this volume.

Apart from contributing a number of new ideas to the debate on art and copyright, this collection of essays presents a comparative approach to the question: it contains commentary on the law and legal tradition of Scandinavia, Britain and the United States. Furthermore, there is a concern in all the essays to find a cure for the anomalies that are evident in copyright law today. Art deserves this, as does copyright, according to its original intention. And while some of the proposed solutions are more radical than others it is generally agreed that copyright exists for the sake of art, not the other way around.

In the first contribution to this volume, 'How to get it Copy-Right', Jens Schovsbo, Professor of Intellectual Property Law at the University of Copenhagen, notes that if there is widespread agreement that copyright is going through a crisis the explanations given are worlds apart. Has the crisis, indeed, arisen because there is too much copyright or because there is too little? To be sure, as Professor Schovsbo demonstrates, copyright law has expanded in every possible sense: in time, territory, scope and subject matter. More seriously a distortion of the copyright system has taken place. The traditional subjects of copyright law, authors, artists and composers, increasingly find themselves beaten aside by media groups and other commercial exploiters of copyright. This affects the very foundation of copyright law. Such extensive exclusive rights as it provides can be justified only with reference to the social and cultural benefits of the objects – literary, artistic and musical works – of copyright. If copyright law has come to serve as a mere convenience for manufacturers of various mundane products the justification for copyright has gone.

Following these reflections on the present state of copyright law, Professor Schovsbo makes the further case that in the digital environment the conceptual framework of copyright law as a system of ownership rights ceases to be adequate. In addition, the founding categories of intellectual property law, such as 'work of authorship', 'invention', and more, have lost clarity and consistency in the process of incorporating more than a century's worth of new technologies. A more suitable approach, it is argued, would therefore be to define and secure a number of

'Users' Rights'. Such Users' Right would add flexibility to the system of copyright; and contribute to the spread of democracy, freedom of information and freedom of expression. This would constitute a step in the right direction.

N55 is a Scandinavian artists' collective with a speculative as well as practical interest in copyright and other intellectual property rights. As is evident in their contribution to this volume, 'On Ownership of Land. On Ownership of Knowledge', and 'Who is LAND for?', they have a theoretical concern with the logical underpinnings of what has been termed 'possessive individualism.'[7] Pointing to absurdities in the notion of individual ownership of what by rights belongs to the *Commons*, their argument unfolds in two directions: in relation to land and to knowledge. In each case the philosopher John Locke's (1632-1704) famous and widely influential labour theory of property is challenged. In *Two Treatises on Civil Government* (1690) John Locke develops the idea that 'whatsoever' a person 'removes out of the state that nature has provided and left it in, he hath mixed his labour with, and joined to it something that is his own, and thereby makes it his property'.[8] This mode of reasoning has come to permeate not only justifications for ownership of land but justifications for ownership of knowledge as well.[9] However, in his theory, Locke makes the stipulation that the establishment of a property right in a piece of land requires that 'enough and as

7. The term 'possessive individualism' derives from C.B. MacPherson's seminal work *The Political Theory of Possessive Individualism. Hobbes to Locke* (London, Oxford, New York: Oxford University Press, 1962). MacPherson's analysis that 'Locke's astonishing achievement was to base the property right on natural right and natural law, and then to remove all the natural law limits from the property right' (199) has been vital in the interpretation of Locke's theory of property.
8. John Locke, *The Second Treatise of Civil Government and A Letter Concerning Toleration. Edited by J. W. Gough*, ed. C.H. Wilson and R.B. McCallum (Oxford: Basil Blackwell, 1948 (1690)), p. 15.
9. The property theory of copyright which is based on the idea of possessive individualism has created the ideological foundation of the Berne Convention and is represented in Article 27 (2) of the Universal Declaration of Human Rights as well.

good [is] left in common for others'.[10] This prerequisite is taken to its strictest extreme by N55: it is argued that any one person's exclusive right in a parcel of land is an inevitable violation of the natural rights of all other persons. 'Enough and as good' is *not* left in common for others to enjoy as long as land and goods continue to be parcelled out. By the same token, ownership of knowledge, for example in the shape of patents, deprives the public of what ought to be a legitimate handling of knowledge and its certain applications.

In a more concrete way, N55 has been faced with a series of dilemmas in the practice of their art. If one acknowledges that creation and invention rely on the existence of a strong public domain it is natural to want to contribute to it in order to prevent this source of creativity and inventiveness from being exhausted. The public domain consists of every intellectual product – literary works, artistic works, design, brands, inventions and more – which, for some reason, is not put under exclusive rights, such as defined by copyright, patent and trademark law. Yet, as N55 and others have discovered, an artwork or an invention is not automatically left in the public domain, even when the originator abstains from claiming his or her exclusive rights in it. It is against the logic of possessive individualism to leave gaps in the global jigsaw puzzle of ownership. Thus, in 1997, when N55 created the artwork 'Dynamic Chair' – a beautiful and, in addition, ergonomical chair – it seemed that the only means of keeping it available to the public would be, absurdly enough, to patent it. Otherwise a person with a commercial interest in the chair might patent it, or in other words claim the exclusive right to its manufacture. In the end, however, the situation was resolved by publishing the manual of the 'Dynamic Chair'. Commercial exploitation of the artwork was not prevented by this; more importantly, the manual could be used as public evidence of invention against any claim to patent it.

10. Locke, p. 15.

When, in 2003, N55 published the *N55 BOOK*, the wish to keep it in the public domain prevailed over the desire to remain in control of its propagation. Accordingly, the book was put out with a copyright notice which substitutes the usual reference to the stipulations of copyright law with the proclamation that:

> the texts and images in *N55 BOOK* may be copied, reproduced and distributed freely. N55 will be thankful to be notified on n55@n55.dk whenever material is being used.

A dilemma faced by all creators is this: when his work is published, it, in a way, starts to belong to everyone. Not even copyright is (as yet) enough to control the reception and treatment a work gets by the public. This dilemma of the artist was here resolved – to the benefit of the public – by trust in the public.

In her piece, 'Artistic Practice and The Integrity of Copyright Law', Fiona Macmillan, Professor of Intellectual Property Law at

Birkbeck College, discusses the protection of works of art under the United Kingdom Copyright Designs and Patents Act 1988. A number of implications of the definition of 'artistic work' according to the 1988 Act are considered. For instance, some works that would be considered 'art' in normal usage are not protected by copyright law because they do not conform properly to the legal description of an 'artistic work'. Conversely, objects that would never pass as art outside the courtroom are successfully protected by copyright law as 'artistic works' because the law prescribes that works should be protected 'irrespective of artistic quality.'

Professor Macmillan demonstrates that the relationship between British copyright law and works of visual art is in fact anomalous seen in the perspective of the general relationship between copyright law and the objects it is designated to protect. It is in the nature of visual art always to test its own limits. What constitutes the category 'visual art' evolves constantly; to fit visual art into the law's definition of 'artistic work' can thus become an art in itself, especially as this category is rather restricted. Furthermore, it seems particularly difficult to maintain a division between fair and unlawful use of existing works of visual art. In principle all works of visual art are derivative: whether this status is subtle or obvious is a matter of artistic style. Finally, a work of art is quite distinct from reproductions of it. An artwork is 'unique' and as such is noticeably more valued and valuable than any reproduction.

'Fair dealing' (a list of uses of a copyright work that the copyright owner cannot prevent) and the 'idea/expression dichotomy' (a distinction between uncopyrightable generic/ universal features of a work and its individual expression, which can be protected) are measures of the law to ensure that future creativity is not stifled by overprotection of the cultural heritage.

However, as Professor Macmillan explains, there are a number of reasons why these measures of the law do not work optimally in relation to art. For example, what is one to do with transitions between two- and three-dimensional works? With works that explicitly play with the cultural significance of copyright and the technologies of reproduction and prolification? And with the fact that one-off artworks have a value in themselves, not only to the extent that they are multiplied?

The role and purpose of copyright law needs constant reassessment. Professor Macmillan concludes her analysis of British copyright protection of art by making some observations as to the rationale of copyright. If it is generally accepted that the role of copyright law is to encourage creativity, it must be shown that it does function to this end. Yet it fails to do so if various contemporary art forms are excluded from the protection of copyright law, and if fair dealing defences as well as the idea/expression dichotomy are not applied appropriately to artistic works. If the law of copyright fails to acknowledge the specific nature of the work of art as an object of protection, the law needs to be amended.

In his article 'Lawyers and Experts in Danish Copyright Infringement Cases', Dr. Morten Rosenmeier discusses the role of expert witnesses. Danish copyright law confronts judges with a paradox of sorts in the stipulation that they are to base their decisions on specialist knowledge. It is impossible for judges – who (for the most part) are trained in the law only – to be experts in each field of knowledge they touch upon when carrying out their duty of passing judgments under Danish law. Yet it is the responsibility of a judge to ensure that the law is upheld in this respect too. Traditionally, the Danish way of resolving this paradox has been to invite expert witnesses. In cases concerning custody, for instance, psychologists are summoned to perform psychological analyses of the parties involved. On the basis of such an expert statement the judge is able to make an informed decision. In cases that require technical expertise, engineers are called in to investigate and explain technical details that enable the judge to rule according to such data. In copyright infringement cases there is a frequent need for aesthetic opinions. These are provided by, for example, architects or designers who are familiar with the aesthetic contexts of copyright items. As experts in arts and crafts, they can report on, say, the degree of creativity and novelty of a work.

Although it seems that the situation may have been resolved by the practice of drawing on expert witnesses, there are a number of problems in the way Danish courts use experts. Expert statements are supposed to offer specialist knowledge upon which the court can base its legal analysis. However, as Dr. Rosenmeier points out, expert witnesses are, as a matter of routine, asked to deliver more than their specialist knowledge in court. They are often asked strictly legal questions, such as whether they consider infringement to have taken place. This is against the law: expert witnesses are under no circumstances to make statements that concern legal issues; they have no competence to do so. Only the expert in law is to arrive at legal conclusions. Therefore, Dr. Rosenmeier declares, it is time to introduce an appropriate division of labour in Danish copyright infringement cases. Judges may judge within the realm of law. Expert witnesses may judge only within their field of expertise.

Marko Karo addresses the topic of art and law in a double optics in 'The Art of Giving and Taking: A Figurative Approach to Copyright Law'. He examines how copyright as a cultural political mechanism conditions contemporary practices of visual art and how an aesthetic evaluative element in legal decisions suggests visual art as a potential source of law. Although the Kantian categories of aesthetics, ethics and jurisprudence are thus transgressed from the beginning, Kant's essay 'On the Wrongfulness of Unauthorized Publication of Books' from 1785 is taken to form the foundation of a provisional perception of law which is better adjusted to the needs of art. In the essay from 1785 Kant draws a sharp distinction between literature and art. Kant excludes art from copyright. However, in the act of doing this, he points to certain features of art that are central to a discussion of how artists' rights are best protected. The current (Anglo-American) property-oriented copyright law may be challenged by what Adorno and Horkheimer in the *Dialectic of Enlightenment* designate as the resistance to the exclusivity and individuality of property that we find in images. Visual signification, as in Kantian phenomenology, works through a process of spectator experience. Copyright law needs to take this in.

A cornerstone of contemporary copyright law is its renunciation of aesthetic judgment. In effect, however, copyright law functions as an institution of 'art criticism': it cements the category of 'Art' by defining it solely in terms of conventional art forms and by delegitimizing artistic practices that rely on copying or imitation as a means of signification. An 'affirmative action' for marginal art would not be helpful here. From the perspective of art, only a narrowing of the term and scope of protection in copyright law would suffice to restrain the monologic tendencies of copyright law. This resistance to monologisation is an inherent element, as Karo points out, of a number of recent artworks that in one way or other involve the use of photography. These are works that illustrate the extent of the potential of art as critique of copyright law. The first example is *Imaginary Homecoming*, by the Finnish photographer Jorma Puranen. *Imaginary Homecoming* was created by rephotographing portraits of Sámi people taken by the French photographer G. Roche in the 1880s on an 'anthropological' expedition; Puranen reexhibits them in the landscape where they were once taken. Puranen's work thus 'steals back' what was 'taken' over a hundred years ago. However, he also enters into a complex play of the 'overappropriation of the real' (as Bernard Edelman terms it) where ownership of the portraits seems to be merely 'colonized' back and forth. The American artist Jeff Koons' sculpture *A String of Puppies* in the exhibition *The Banality Show* is the second example. The sculpture was a three-dimensional reworking of a photograph by the professional photographer Art Rogers. In *Rogers* v. *Koons* (1992) Koons was found guilty of having infringed Rogers' copyright. Koons' claim that his sculpture was a parody, and therefore under 'fair use', was dismissed by the court: Koons work was found to be nothing more and nothing less than an unauthorized reproduction of Rogers' photograph. A third example is the Situationist-inspired French artists Pierre Huyghe and Philipe Parreno who created their work, *No Ghost Just a Shell*, by purchasing the copyright to a generic cartoon character, Ann Lee, and then inviting other artists to supply personality, history, context and so forth.

Karo's discussion of these artworks reveal that the transgressive nature of the gift rather than the subversive act of theft (as explored by appropriation artists, mainly in the 1980s) seems to be the more valid mode of artistic criticism for our day. That is art's contribution to copyright law.

Simon Stokes is both a practitioner of and a commentator on copyright law. His contribution to this book is a presentation of the major issues of contemporary British copyright protection of art. He focuses on the economic rights of artists and discusses in particular how the law of copyright categorises artistic works. In its definition of 'artistic works' the British Copyright Designs and Patents Act 1988 outlines a number of subcategories, such as graphic work, photographs and sculptures. The legal meaning of these art formes does not always spring directly from their meaning in the common use of the terms. Stokes, therefore, goes through case law to illustrate what courts have designated as such works and what has been excluded form copyright protection. One court, for example, had to deal with the question of whether the mould to make a Frisbee would qualify as an engraving.

A number of criteria for protection are discussed. Under British Copyright Law, as under most other national laws of copyright, a work must be 'original' to be eligible for protection. In Britain, however, the level of originality is very low. As case law shows, only a minimum of skill and labour is required, such as pushing the button of an automatic camera. A further criterion for protection is that a work has fixation. As it is, the criteria for protection constitute a number of problems for contemporary artists. Their works may not easily fall under the legal category of 'artistic work.' This is the case for, say, ready-mades and conceptual art. Consequently, artists have no protection against commercial exploitation (in, for example, advertisements) of their works. Conversely, there are branches of contemporary art such as 'appropriation art', which are based on taking previous works and turning them into something new. Parodies may also fall under this class of works. British Copyright Law is not well-equipped to handle these: there is no specific permission to create parodies, as there is for example in French law, and there are no guide lines to distinguish appropriation for the sake of art from downright infringement.

All the essays in this collection suggest that copyright is presently going through some sort of crisis. There are problems with the classificatory system of copyright, the property-orientation of copyright law and the shrinking public domain. What is also clear is that the current crisis is being exacerbated by the Internet. No doubt copyright has gone through crises before: the invention of photography in the mid-nineteenth century and of the photocopier in the late twentieth, for example, seriously challenged the copyright system. In each case copyright law adapted to the new order. This may happen again. Yet there are signs that, this time, the scale of the technological rupture—the change from an analog to a digital order—is without precedent. The logic of copyright is under threat, and the law may find itself powerless to respond, or to assert effectively its claim to protect that right. The most interesting developments may be found among those who seek an alternative to copyright: the 'Free Art License' and the 'Creative Commons License'[11], for example, seek to provide some protection for works of art without restricting access to it. Here it is important to realize that such moves are not necessarily 'anti-copyright'. Rather they propose a more flexible approach, above all in their determination that the rights-holders – whether artists or owners or distributors – ought not to be allowed to deny or abrogate the legitimate rights of the public.

11. See www.artlibre.org and www.creativecommons.org.

How to get it Copy-Right

Jens Schovsbo *

CRISIS: WHAT CRISIS?

The law of copyright is often said to be in a state of 'crisis'. It has been in crisis before and it will probably be in crisis again. However, this time it seems that the crisis is of a different, more existential nature than before. Thus, one group of commentators says that the crisis has arisen because copyright law is too restrictive, so information is not accessible. Another group of commentators says that the problem is that copyright law is too weak, and people have too much access to information. The group saying that copyright is too restrictive seems to have won the ear of the public. The group which says that copyright is too weak has won over legislators and taken possession of the rules. It is impossible to satisfy one side without disappointing the other.

General scepticism about copyright law is not limited to internet cafés and teenage culture, but is much more widespread, cf. the dissenting opinion of Justice Breyer in the US Supreme Court decision in *Eldred v Ashcroft*, given on 15 January 2003, in which, with reference to the extension of copyright from 50 to 70 years following the death of the author, he said:

> It is easy to understand how the statute might benefit the private financial interests of corporations or heirs who own existing copyrights. But I cannot find any constitutionally legitimate, copyright-related way in which the statute will benefit the public. Indeed, in respect to existing works, the

* LL.M, Dr.jur., Professor of intellectual property law, University of Copenhagen

serious public harm and the virtually nonexistent public benefit could not be more clear.

The idea of copyright

Copyright law ought to serve the interests of society. Traditionally, copyright policy has been governed by the need to protect the interests of authors. Implicitly, the interests of authors have been presumed to equal the interests of society at large. During the last twenty years the copyright system has developed from being a rather obscure area of the law into a system of central importance. Most of the so-called 'New economy' is based on copyright protection of music, games, films and computer programs and databases. This development can be seen both from an economic point of view and from a broader, cultural perspective. The grant of copyright entails social costs and the costs tend to increase with stronger protection. Somewhere in the enormous expansion of copyright which has taken place in the last twenty years copyright law has lost its touch with its basic rationale: to serve the interests of society. Instead of expanding in response to the needs of society, copyright law has gathered its own momentum and is developing and expanding according to its own internal 'proprietary' logic.

The expansion of copyright

Today copyright law has expanded in every dimension: time (from 50 to 70 years of protection), territory (the EU, the whole world (via the WTO Agreements) and into hyperspace), scope (stronger exclusive rights) and subject matter covered. The last dimension – subject matter – is evident when one looks at present copyright legislation. At one end of the copyright spectrum there are the entertainment and IT industries, with their claims for the protection of their investments in films, music, computer programs and databases etc., and at the other end there are the traditional originators of works, such as authors, composers, painters etc., with claims to protection based on their personal rights. This latter group is the standard-bearer of the ideology of copyright and the core norms and rules of copyright, while the former group reflects the economic reality of copyright. The growth of copyright law in recent years has largely been based on regard for the classical copyright virtues, but the effect has been to strengthen the commercial and industrial side of copyright. This development is still in progress as is demonstrated clearly in the new European Directive on the enforcement of intellectual property rights.

The legislative eagerness to protect the interests of producers has led to a distortion of the copyright system. In this connection, it is not only users of copyright materials who may feel that their interests are disregarded, it is also the traditional authors of works. It has never been particularly lucrative to be an author, composer or playwright. It will be no easier to become rich in the future. Developments in contractual practice show a clear trend for acquirers of rights, often major media groups, to try to secure broader and more comprehensive rights than previously. They often get their way. There are more authors than there are publishers, and publishers' contract proposals are often accepted without discussion, let alone negotiation. Copyright law has not traditionally been concerned with this. The legislation has traditionally contained some rules and principles, generally default rules, but the prevailing view has been that there should be freedom of contract, and the parties should be left to themselves. The time is probably ripe for a reassessment of this view. There is a precedent for this in Germany, where a new law '*zur Stärkung der vertraglichen Stellung von Urhebern und ausübenden Künstlern*' entered into force on 1st July 2002. Under this law, the author obtains an inalienable right to reasonable remuneration. This is normally understood to be the remuneration which is fixed in collective agreements between opposing organisations. However, it is interesting that the purpose of the law is not merely to prevent injustice, but is based on the view that developments in contractual practice have meant that the expansion of the sphere of copyright has not sufficiently benefited the authors. Commercial exploiters of copyright have grabbed a share of the cake which was intended for the originators of works. This view, which is undoubtedly correct, illustrates how it is impossible to separate the formal ownership of copyright, the rights given by the law, from the material aspects, reflected in the development of the market. Modern developments in copyright law should reflect all aspects of the contemporary reality of copyright issues.

The weight given to the interests of commercial exploiters of copyright in this expansion of the sphere of copyright law has not merely been relevant to the sharing out of the profits between originators and exploiters. This development concerns the purpose and ideology of copyright and, in the long run, it affects the very justification for copyright. As the late Professor of Intellectual Property Law, Mogens Koktvedgaard, describes it:

> The whole system of copyright is effectively based on a fundamental lie, in which fine words are used to conjure up the illusion that copyright protects literary and artistic works and serves the higher interests of the fine arts etc. But the truth is that today the law is primarily there to protect the commercial interests of the providers of various products and services, and has no regard either for the quality of these products and services or their social justification.[1]

GETTING THE BALANCE RIGHT

Today, if one looks at the legislation, one cannot avoid the conclusion that copyright has reached the end of the road. It is simply not feasible to stretch any further the exclusive rights given by copyright. With the adoption of the Information Society Directive (2001/29/EC on the harmonisation of certain aspects of copyright and related rights in the information society) copyright law has gone beyond its traditional sphere by including the protection of Technological Protection Measures (TPM) and Digital Rights Management systems (DRM) within the scope of the exclusive rights granted. With such instruments at hand, it is increasingly being left to the owner of copyright to decide the form and content of protection by, for example, laying down the conditions for access to internet sites in 'click-wrap' copyright agreements. The traditional exclusive rights given by copyright

1. Festschrift for Gunnar Karnell, 1999, p. 344.

were granted in order to protect the originator of a work against anonymous exploitation by third parties. When there is on-line usage, the owner of the rights and the user of those rights can be in direct contact with one another. Their relationship is direct and contractual, and the need for an exclusive right to regulate the relationship is rather different than in a traditional environment where the rightholder is often unable to look after himself and his rights, and is in need of legal protection. In the new on-line, click-wrap environment it is rather the user who needs to have his rights safeguarded by the law.

Users' Rights?

The task of copyright law in this on-demand, individualized scenario consists of ensuring that the general concerns which were the original core of copyright law, for example determining what can be subject to copyright and the duration of protection, are not eroded by individual licence agreements. The balance must be maintained. The interests of society must prevail.
The traditional idea of copyright, as protecting the rights of the originator of a work, is not a suitable starting point, as this will certainly lead to a strengthening of the rights of the copyright owner and not to the broader perception needed, aimed at a solution which is best from a more general point of view. There is a need to break with the systematic logic of 'ownership' of rights which has characterised copyright hitherto. There needs to be a counterbalance to the ideology of 'ownership' which has dominated copyright until now.

A suitable candidate for this counterbalance could be a clearer emphasis in copyright law on the interests of Users. Such 'Users' Rights' could include e.g. a right to 'Information use' (i.e. no copyright protection of information as such), 'Democratic use' (i.e. copyright is not to be used to suppress opinions, including criticism and parodies), 'transformative use' (i.e. copyright is not to be used to bar works which add considerable value compared to the existing stock of works and which do not merely imitate existing works) and, lastly, a right to 'reasonable commercial use'.[2]

The introduction of such a Charter of Users' Rights would require a firm approach to the restrictions on copyright found in the copyright Treaties and in national legislation e.g. in Chapter 2 of the Danish Copyright Act. Consideration for Users' Rights means that the system should be made more flexible. In traditional European law there has been reluctance to adopt the 'fair use' rules known in American law. This reluctance should be reviewed. The catalogue of exceptions listed in the Information Society Directive is not the way forward. In spite of the model of the Information Society Directive, there is already a growing measure of openness in the system. Competition law always requires openness, as do the rules in the EC Treaty on the free movement of goods. The rules and principles on the freedom of expression is another area to be build in to copyright. These considerations, and others which will arise, ought to be integrated in copyright law in the form of special provisions to be implemented in order to give an overall balance between consideration for originators of works and consideration for users of works.

CAN THE SYSTEM COPE?

There may be scope for even more fundamental thinking about copyright law and whether it is appropriately structured. The continental European system of intellectual property law, of which Denmark is a part, is based on conventional categorical thinking derived from German romantic jurisprudence (Joseph Kohler and others) of the late the nineteenth century. What is decisive for whether some created work or invention should be protected under one or another set of rules is an abstract classification of the object to be protected. If it is a literary or artistic 'work', the relevant pigeon-hole is copyright law; if it is an 'invention' it belongs

2. For more on Users' Rights see Thomas Riis and Jens Schovsbo, 'Users' rights: Reconstructing Copyright Policy on Utilitarian Grounds', European Intellectual Propery Review (forthcoming).

under patent law; trade marks belong under trade mark law, and so on. Everything is controlled by categories. The choice of pigeon-hole determines the conditions for obtaining protection and the rules governing the content and duration of that protection. This system is linked to the traditional balance between the conflicting interests of the owners of rights and of society as a whole. Copyright is clearly intended to protect the author and copyright protection was developed to meet the needs of the author, as the creator of an original work, to be given specially comprehensive protection for his intellectual ideas. The central principles of copyright, involving a literary or artistic 'work', 'originality' and an 'author' (author or artist), are mutually dependent and cohesive. From a general legal point of view this works well, as long as there is a cohesion between the ideal world of the system which lies behind the rules and the real world. There will be such cohesion as long as the categorical approach helps to identify the circumstances which can appropriately fall within the copyright system, and as long as these circumstances are sufficiently uniform as to be reasonably subject to the same treatment and give rise to the same exclusive rights and so forth. The expansion of copyright has meant that this internal cohesion is no longer evident. This can be disguised to some extent, by developing special rules, as has been done for computer programmes and databases, and by adjusting the conceptual framework, as with the concept of the level of creativity in relation to applied art (i.e. 'designs'). However, one cannot avoid the fundamental question of whether the structure of copyright law is appropriate for contemporary needs. The question is important. The current structure is impractical, and not merely because of the lack of clarity of its central principles. For example, in design, it is not clear whether there should be a special standard for the level of creativity to be obtained or whether such a stipulation should be regarded as included in the requirement for originality and, if so, whether this is an EU-harmonised concept.

The existing structure is based on the classic doctrine of classifying the object to be protected and prevents the development of copyright law towards becoming a more open system taking into account other interests of society, such as users' interests, to a greater extent than today. As pointed out by Rosenmeier, consideration should be given to whether, at least for certain kinds of works, protection should be freed from the traditional approach of categories of protected objects and that instead should be granted from an investment point of view.[3] Instead of looking at abstract concepts and deducing legal consequences from them, one should look at the practical realities and provide protection not only for 'art and literature', 'computer programmes', 'concepts', 'broadcasts', 'films' and 'product design' and so forth.

THE FUTURE

It is becoming more and more difficult to find the balance between what people regard as right and the right granted by copyright law. The question is not so much *whether* there must be radical changes, but rather *what* these changes should be and *how* they should be implemented. The changes required should not merely aim to improve the existing system, but should bring about a root and branch reform. It was with good reason that Thomas Riis raised the battle cry for new values in copyright law under the banner: 'Rebuild copyright law on a utilitarian foundation'.[4] If copyright law is to survive, it must ensure that it serves the interests of society, and not just those of the owners of rights.

3. Festschrift for Mogens Koktvedgaard (Copenhagen, 2003), pp. 502-505.
4. Festschrift for Mogens Koktvedgaard (Copenhagen, 2003), p. 445 et seq.

On Ownership of Land. On Ownership of Knowledge

*N55**

Logic

Logical relations are the most basic and most overlooked phenomenon we know. Nothing of which we can talk rationally can exist, can be identified or referred to, except through its logical relations to other things. Logic is necessary relations between different factors, and factors are what exist by the force of those relations. The decisive thing about logical relations is that they can not be reasoned. Nevertheless, they do constitute conditions necessary for any description, because they can not be denied without rejecting the factors of the relations. Persons are, for example, totally different from their bodies. Persons can go for a walk and they can make decisions. Bodies can not do that. Nevertheless, we can not refer to persons without referring to their bodies. If we say: here we have a person, but he or she unfortunately is lacking a body, it does not make sense. Persons are totally different from the concrete situations they are in. Nevertheless, we can not refer to persons without referring to the situations they are in. If we say: here we have a person, but this person has never been in a concrete situation, it does not make sense. Language is totally different from reality. Nevertheless, we have to perceive language as something that can be used to talk about reality. If we say: here we have a language, but this

* N55 is a Scandinavian artist collective based in Copenhagen, www.n55.dk.

language can not be used to talk about reality, it does not make sense. Logical relations have decisive significance. The absence of logical relations would mean that nothing could be of decisive significance: as long as one does not contradict oneself nor is inconsistent with facts, any point of view may be as good as the next, one can say and mean anything. Logical relations are conditions for talking rationally together. The part of the world we can talk rationally about, can thus be defined as the part we can talk about using logical relations. But we do not have any reason to assume that the world is identical with what we can talk rationally about. Logic is something more basic than language. Logical relations are what makes language a language and what assigns meaning to words. Therefore, it is impossible to learn a language, without learning to respect logical relations. But as we grow up and learn to master language, logical relations are not present on a conscious level. If we are conscious of logical relations, it is possible for us to decide whether something is right or wrong and not to allow ourselves to be ruled by for example habitual conceptions and subjective opinions.

PERSONS

A person can be described in an infinite number of ways. None of these descriptions can be completely adequate. We therefore can not describe precisely what a person is. Whichever way we describe a person, we do however have the possibility to point out necessary relations between persons and other factors. We have to respect these relations and factors in order not to contradict ourselves and in order to be able to talk about persons in a meaningful way. One necessary relation is the logical relation between persons and bodies. It makes no sense to refer to a person without referring to a body. If we for example say: here we have a person, but he or she does not have a body, it does not make sense. Furthermore, there are necessary relations between persons and the rights of persons. Persons should be treated as persons and therefore as having rights. If we deny this assertion it goes wrong: here is a person, but this person should not be treated as a person, or: here is a person, who should be treated as a person, but not as having rights. Therefore we can only talk about persons in a way that makes sense if we know that persons have rights.

Concentrations of power

Concentrations of power do not always respect the rights of persons. If one denies this fact one gets: concentrations of power always respect the rights of persons. This does not correspond with our experiences. Concentrations of power characterize our society. Concentrations of power force persons to concentrate on participating in competition and power games, in order to create a social position for themselves. Concurrently with the concentrations of power dominating our conscious mind and being decisive to our situations, the significance of our fellow humans diminishes. And our own significance becomes the significance we have for concentrations of power, the growth of concentrations of power, and the conflicts of concentrations of power.

It is clear that persons should be consciously aware of the rights of persons and therefore must seek to organize the smallest concentrations of power possible.

Ownership of land

It is a habitual conception that ownership of land is acceptable. Most societies are characterized by the convention of ownership. But if we claim the ownership of land, we also say that we have more right to parts of the surface of the earth, than other persons have.

We know that persons should be treated as persons and therefore as having rights. If we say here is a person who has rights, but this person has no right to stay on the surface of the earth, it does not make sense. If one does not accept that persons have the right to stay on the surface of the earth, it makes no sense to talk about rights at all. If we try to defend ownership of land using language in a rational way it goes wrong. The only way of defending this ownership is by the use of power and force. No persons have more right to land than other persons, but concentrations of power use force to maintain the illusion of ownership of land.

PATENTS – OWNERSHIP OF OBJECTIVE KNOWLEDGE

Science is about making right assertions. Right assertions represent objective knowledge. Objective knowledge is something which can't be denied meaningfully, if we want to talk rationally together. Objective knowledge can be knowledge about facts: at four o'clock they sat down and did this, or this mountain is 3000 meters high. Objective knowledge can also be knowledge about logical relations.

To take a patent on for example knowledge about the human genome or a new type of medicine, is to claim ownership of objective knowledge. This means that some persons claim the ownership of logical relations and knowledge about facts. This ownership means that other persons must, for example, pay in order to use objective knowledge, or that other persons are not allowed at all to use it. If we claim a patent to objective knowledge, we also say that some persons can use logical relations and facts and some can not: Here we have a person, who should be treated as a person and therefore as having rights, but this person is not allowed to use logical relations or knowledge about facts. It does not make sense to claim ownership of objective knowledge. If we try to defend ownership of objective knowledge using language in a rational way it goes wrong. The only way one can defend ownership of objective knowledge is by using power and force. No persons have more right to use logical relations or knowledge about facts than other persons, but concentrations of power use force to maintain the illusion of ownership of objective knowledge.

MANUAL FOR LAND

INTRODUCTION:

LAND gives access to land. Any person can stay in LAND and use it.

CONSTRUCTION:

LAND is constructed from pieces of land in different places in the world. The various parts are added to LAND by persons who guarantee that anybody can stay in LAND and use it. Any person can initiate expansions of LAND. The geographical positions of LAND can be found in Manual for LAND. The manual is continuously updated at www.N55.dk/LAND.html. A current version can also be obtained by contacting N55.

USING LAND:

Any person can use LAND. Attention is directed to the logical relation between persons and the rights of persons. Persons should be treated as persons and therefore as having rights. If we deny this assertion it goes wrong: here is a person, but this person should not be treated as a person, or: here is a person, who should be treated as a person, but not as having rights. Therefore we can only talk about persons in a way that makes sense if we know that persons have rights.

EXPANDING LAND:

LAND can be expanded by anybody who wants to add pieces of land to LAND. Formally, the parts of LAND remain the property of the persons participating in this way, but they guarantee that any person can stay in LAND and use it.

By informing N55 of the position, a cairn will be put out to mark the place and the position will be distributed through the manual.

CAIRNS:

All parts of LAND are marked with a cairn (height 1 m). The cairns have a frame of stainless acid resistant steel and built-in tanks of PE-plastic. The tanks are equipped with a transparent lid of polycarbonate, tightened with rubber strips.

There is a manual and other equipment in the tanks. Apart from this, the configuration and size of the cairns will be modified according to the sites and their requirements.

MAINTENANCE:
LAND is maintained by persons using it. The manuals placed in the cairns will be updated continuously.

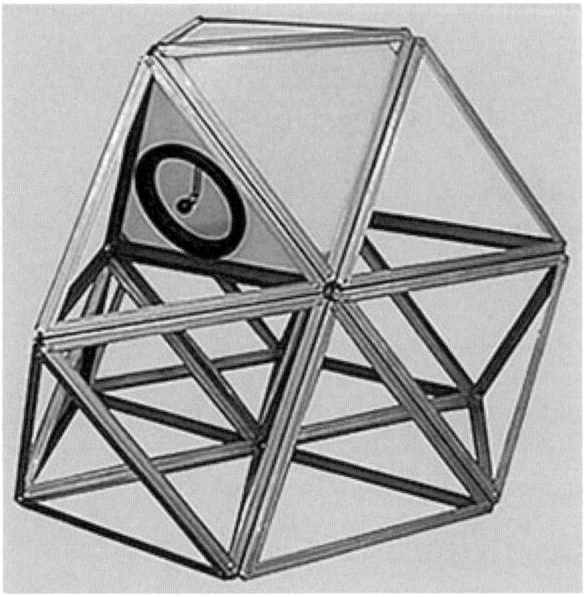

CURRENT LAND POSITIONS:
N 70° 09' 42,5" E 019° 56' 41,3"
N 41° 53' 03,4" E 087° 46' 06,8"
N 33° 10' 43,9" E -117° 14' 26,7"
N 44° 36' 03,2" E 001° 15' 04,6"
N 55° 14' 24,8" E 011° 56' 22,3"
N 52° 6' 04,5" E 005° 3' 04,5"
N 47° 19' 42,4" E 009° 24' 31,6"
N 52° 18' 19,7" E 005° 32' 11,7"
N 41° 47' 58" E 087° 36' 23"
N 57° 10' 43,3" E 010° 05' 13,1"
N 55° 58' 10,2" E 013° 45' 16,2"
N 57° 20' 04,5" E 010° 30' 56,5"
N 56° 59' 55" E 009° 19' 33,7"
N 43° 17' 48,1" E 000° 22' 21"
N 45° 09' 36" E 029° 41' 24"
N 29° 43' 29,1" W 095° 20' 32,6"

Who is Land for?
About Position:
N 41° 47' 58", E 87° 36' 23"

N55, B. Bloom, D. Wang and S. Orman

Brett Bloom lives in Chicago and works with Temporary Services (www.temporaryservices.org)

The interview was conducted in 2002 and includes a comment by Dan S. Wang and Sarah Van Orman, who included a piece of land in LAND the same year.

BRETT BLOOM:

I want to take time to discuss the real world barriers that exist in realizing projects like LAND. LAND is a project that could potentially spread until all land is freed up and the project is no longer necessary – that seems to be a logical, conceptual conclusion. I don't think this will happen because of the massive power structures that stand in the way.

Who is LAND for? If LAND is contained within larger nation states that are anti-immigration, paranoid about foreign nationals launching clandestine attacks, limit the amount of time a foreign national can spend in the country or are just not open societies, then how can LAND be available to everyone?

Isn't LAND incredibly vulnerable to the whims of nation states that decide whether or not to tolerate LAND and access to LAND?

N55:

LAND is a way of effecting some real changes in a realistic way. To change legislation or government is not realistic at the moment. However, if legislation and governments were receptive to logic, they would have to accept the following argument against ownership of land:

It is a habitual conception that ownership of land is acceptable. Most societies are characterized by the convention of ownership. But if we claim the ownership of land, we also say that we have more right to parts of the surface of the earth than other persons have. We know that persons should be treated as persons and therefore as having rights. If we say here is a person who has rights, but this person has no right to stay on the surface of the earth, it does not make sense. If one does not accept that persons have the right to stay on the surface of the earth, it makes no sense to talk about rights at all. If we try to defend ownership of land using language in a rational way it goes wrong. The only way to defend ownership is to use power and force. No persons have more right to land than other persons, but concentrations of power use force to maintain the illusion of ownership of land.

Here the focus is on what logic and language can teach us, and not on what has been learned from different ideologies and political systems. This makes it possible to reject ownership on an objective basis, meaning on a basis that cannot be denied meaningfully.

When we talk about LAND as well as about ownership in general, some habitual thinking is challenged. And that has an effect. Attention is directed at something that is often overlooked. LAND represents a marked difference from habitual thinking about property: ownership normally entitles people to expel others from land, use of things, etc. By reducing things to being property, one is creating the illusion of an absence of relations between the thing and other persons, and between persons in relation to the thing. Through LAND, these relations are made visible. Slowly, other forms of behaviour are taking place.

Of course one of the ways LAND functions is by making the existing constraints visible. For example: transgressing national borders without permission. These constraints exist not only on the practical level of immigration and so on, but also in our thinking. The absence of the conventional rules of ownership in LAND creates a general confusion. We no longer know exactly what we are expected to do and what the limits are, and so we have to start thinking for ourselves.

BB:
What is the difference between LAND and land-rights movements that forcefully claim land for landless persons? Isn't LAND coming from a position of privilege and wealth when we have to rely on the generosity of landowners and people with the power of private property?

N55:
To pretend to step out of our western, privileged position would be hypocritical. LAND is one attempt among many practices in the world that question and undermine structures of power and ownership. Although most people in Europe and the US are not in desperate need of land or food, we are in desperate need of diversity and respect of the fundamental rights of persons and in desperate need to minimize power concentration. The latter needs we probably share with most land-right movements that seize land, like those in Brazil, for example the Landless Workers Movement MST.

LAND is one link in a general attempt to live with as small concentrations of power as possible. A relatively wealthy and privileged position provides a surplus that isn't the worst starting point to try and change things. You don't have to be desperately poor to be legitimate in your wish for changes. The important thing is that one sees how basic needs and concentrations of power are connected. And that one tries to change that, wherever one lives.

It has been surprising to find out that many people in Europe and the US of small income actually own land. Earlier, this distribution of land to many small holders might have been a way of securing basic needs for people, replacing former systems where a few wealthy persons owned large estates. However the large estates still remain today, and the decisive chunks of land, for example in cities, are not accessible to others than very wealthy and powerful people. Capitalism has created new monopolies.

Those who participate in expanding LAND, use their ownership to guarantee others access. This is not just private charity. It is a step in a longer process and an experiment that involves taking some risks. The formal owners for example risk trouble with their local authorities.

BB: What are the channels of distribution of the information about participating in LAND? Who has access to this information and who is participating? Is this just being presented in art contexts, journals, and the art world or is there a conscious effort to spread information well beyond these constraints?

N55:

We try to take care that the information is done in ways that don't contradict the contents of LAND. We do not seek out certain media, they approach us. We distribute LAND information through manuals in public places, through the website, exhibitions, and lectures, and the manuals are available for passers-by on the LAND sites. It has also been distributed in newspapers. Through word of mouth, and other ways, an increasing number of people know about LAND. It has existed for little more than two years.

N55's role so far has been to take care of the manual and website and distribute the information that is submitted to us. If other people find other ways of distributing the knowledge of LAND, this is fine. We'd very much like it to grow out of our control.

BB:

You refuse to create concentrations of power or ideological positions with your work. I think that this confuses people. I think people expect you to be solution providers (because of the way they are taught to perceive work that seems to be like yours) – that you will give them answers to all the world's ills in the form of a new totalizing ideology. They look for a purity of intention and for purity in how you live your lives. People also have a strong reaction because they think that you are trying to tell them how to live or to impose your ideas on them. Could you talk some more about these and other habitual conceptions that people have and how to work towards breaking them down so people can really see logical relations and understand their importance?

N55:

It seems you describe two opposite types of reaction against us, or people who propose changes of some kind. One is that we don't provide enough solutions, and another is that we impose our solutions on others.

Confusing people for a second is not necessarily a bad thing. This makes them leave the safe grounds of habitual conceptions, ideologies, etc., for a moment. Maybe they even start to think for themselves. We don't try to impose any ideology on other persons. Or religion. We don't try to impose any ideologies, whether political or religious, on other persons. Ideologies or religions are not about respecting persons, persons' rights or logical relations in general. Ideologies and religions are about using power, even if they contradict what we know is right, to force ideas on persons. Ideologies and religions can only exist because of power.

What we are talking about is what any person in the world shares already: namely, the ability to use language, and respect logical relations and facts, and hereby conditions for description. Everyone who can speak a language shares this ability, although it is not always used. In our work we try to take consequences of the things we know and the things we learn, in our daily lives. And then we try to communicate these experiences to other persons. If we cannot do this, we are not allowed to communicate at all. Of course our practice is critical, and the consequence for other persons that really understand what we are doing, might be that they would like to change things in their lives. But this is called communication. It's not about imposing anything. If persons change their lives because they get consciously aware of logical relations, it's fine with us. But you cannot force other persons to understand. So we are quite confident that we don't impose anything on other persons. Maybe we should try to talk more thoroughly about what logical relations means. Most discussions are dominated by different ideologies and subjective opinions. We repeat habitual conceptions to each other. The question of who is right often gets distorted into a question of who has the power. But, there is a level at which things are not a matter of power games or subjective opinions. At this level things are simply right or wrong. This level is what can be described as logical relations, or conditions for descriptions. It is what we use all the time when we speak, or when we act in relation to our surroundings. In trying to formulate right sentences or even sentences that deliberately distort reality any person demonstrates an excellent knowledge of language and reality. Having this knowledge is the same as knowing logical relations, without which, language breaks down. With this knowledge, it is possible to say correct sentences about what one has been eating today or about politics. And it is possible to say whether an assertion is based on facts and logic or on subjective opinions only. For example it is possible to find out whether the sentence: "rights are something which is given to persons at certain times and in certain political systems, and which do not exist in others", is correct, simply by looking at what we mean by the word "rights". If it isn't something persons have, then what is it? Can we talk of persons without assuming that persons have rights, and still maintain our understanding of what a person is? And further, if we by "rights" do not understand a right to be on the surface of the earth, it makes no sense to talk of rights at all.

There are of course many issues within this area that can be discussed and where to some degree cultural differences play a role. The thing we are concerned with here is a basic level of language, where language stops working if we don't respect certain factors like "persons" and "rights", and certain relations such as those between words and that which the words are about. Other logical relations are relations between persons and concrete situations, between persons and bodies, and in geometry, between points and distances. Logic is necessary relations between different factors, and factors are what exist by the force of those relations. Formal logic is another example of logical relations. And there are probably many which we do not know.

Experience tells us that concentrations of power do not always respect the rights of persons. And sometimes a large concentration of power is necessary to protect some persons' rights. The only thing we can conclude from this is that persons ought to try to organize the smallest concentrations of power possible. Still, this is decisive to our work. And although they are on another level than that of logical consistency, our different things and activities are important ways of proposing concrete changes. The manuals convey information on how they were made and then it's up to other people if they want to make use of the systems, get inspired, ignore them, laugh at them, copy them or improve them. N55 experience could be seen as an open source. You can learn from it or not learn from it. LAND seems to be an instance where many people can connect. The contradictions of land ownership are quite obvious to many. And LAND provides an opportunity to make experiments with ownership without having to subscribe to an ideology.

About position: N 41° 47' 58", E 87° 36' 23"

By Dan S. Wang and Sarah Van Orman, Hyde Park, Chicago, July 2002.

The analysis summed up in the term "logical relations" presents one way of proofing courses of action against falling into bureaucratic modes of exercising power. That is to say, "logical relations" offers a way of thinking about living and the exercises of power necessitated by living that is free from the tendency to concentrate power. We find N55's concept of logical relations compelling and significant, and wish to contribute to the further development of this thought.

Because we already mostly agree with the theory, we believe the best way to contribute is to help with the practical experimentation. We are in a position to expand LAND, and want to catalyze it by adding a more experimental element to what's already happening with the project. By "experimental" we mean an intensively observed element. The goal is to discern the contradictions and problems of LAND as the project is conducted in this particular situation. Similarly, we also hope to identify the strengths of this project, the promising elements, the unforeseen successes. In other words, we participate in this project with the hope of taking the project to its limits at the points where it is bounded, and beyond, at the points where it is not. We hold title to a (comparatively) small parcel of land adjacent to our condominium property. It is a narrow strip about 3.5 meters wide and 20 meters long. The first two years of ownership netted for

Sarah (who has taken charge of the reclamation) many hours of clearing scrub and stumps, cleaning out trash, glass, and broken concrete. We now have enough space for a garden and for parking our car. The problem is that other people have occasionally parked their car there, too, without our knowledge or agreement. Given not only our possessive impulses, but also the real record of violent and unregulated anti-social activity in our immediate half-block vicinity (a shooting, a mob action, a burglary, a home intrusion, an assault, all in the last two years), we have been very protective against any unknown users of this space. These situations have resulted in several personal confrontations, one of which for reasons of escalation involved the police.

Our interest in expanding LAND stems from this situation of mutual encroachment by strangers, we who acquired title to the parcel, and they who see opportunity to use it without taking care of it (for example, littering and dumping on the site has been a constant problem). Thus, perhaps contrary to past expansions motivated by a wish to make available privately held space, and possibly undermine the root culture that enables private property as a whole, this particular expansion of LAND rests on a hyper-local fact of excluding and controlling users. We therefore initiate this expansion of LAND in order to heighten the contradiction between our values and ideals, and the real and perceived demands of an actual situation. The goal is to study this contradiction and move to resolve it productively, so that a lesson may be learned and applied in similar situations elsewhere.

POSITION: N 41° 47' 58", E 87° 36' 23"

Dan S. Wang, December 2002.

It took a few days for us to notice the emptiness. And later, the scattered nuts and bolts.

LAND is available for use. A beautiful 1 m high cairn supplied by N55 marks LAND. But not here, not anymore.

Our fault. We don't like tying things down unless we absolutely have to. First our watering wand and then later our cooler were stolen from our porch this past summer; they weren't exactly hidden, and we knew quite well (from experience) the possibility that they would be taken. So, out with the 20 yearold cooler inherited from my parents, and in with a better performing, $14.95 cooler from Target. Call it a benefit of global overproduction. We can afford to indulge in recreational petty theft, from the victim's side of things. Well, if we leave this... how long before it's nicked? The moulded plastic chairs are still there. It's entirely possible that somebody liked the cairn so much that they just had to have it. But somehow we find it more appealing that the physical symbol binding this parcel of earth to the other parcels comprising LAND met with a fate in keeping with the way space is frequently used around where we live – as a zone for legally ambiguous scavenging: it's there, take it, and use it to get something else.

LAND remains, but unmarked, uncoded, and mostly undifferentiated from the space surrounding it. No cairn on LAND, only a compost bin.

Artistic Practice and the Integrity of Copyright Law

Fiona Macmillan[*]

Introduction

It is hardly contentious to suggest that the relationship between copyright law and creativity is somewhat uncertain. Among the myriad reasons for this, three stand out. The first is that creativity is protected under copyright law only where its product falls within one of the categories of 'copyright work'. Secondly, tensions between creativity and copyright protection result from the way in which copyright must relate to the creative process both by protecting creative output and by allowing the use of that creative output for the purpose of creating other works. Thirdly, it might be argued with some plausibility that copyright's focus is the protection, not of primary creative works, but of derivative or entrepreneurial works. Thus, the authors of primary creative works, such as literary, dramatic, musical and artistic works, derive less economic benefit from the copyright system than the 'authors' of sound recordings, films, broadcasts and published editions.[1] This is consistent with the proposition that a primary

* Professor of Law, Birkbeck College, University of London

1. See R Towse, *Creativity, Incentive and Reward: An Economic Analysis of Copyright and Culture in the Information Age* (London: Edward Elgar Publishing, 2001), esp chs 6 & 8, in which it is argued that copyright generates little income for most creative artists. Nevertheless, Towse suggests that copyright is valuable to creative artists for reasons of status and control of their work.

function of copyright law is communicative.[2] Yet, it leaves the question of what copyright law might be attempting to achieve in relation to the primary creative works in something of a state of limbo.

This paper examines the question of the relationship between copyright law and that form of creativity that leads to the production of works of visual art. As the paper will attempt to show, in many respects this relationship is anomalous when compared to copyright's treatment of other forms of creativity. A reasonable indication of this might be derived from a consideration of this comparison in the light of the three factors mentioned above. First, like other forms of creative output, works of visual art must fit within the copyright definition of 'artistic work'. Compared to copyright's definition of other forms of creative output, however, this definition is highly specific and prescriptive. Secondly, as in relation to other forms of creative productivity, the copyright protection of works of visual art searches for a balance between protecting creativity and permitting its use in further creative works. However, this balance seems particularly problematic in relation to artistic works – not least because of the growth of artistic practices and traditions that focus on this creative tension. Thirdly, works of visual art seem to raise different issues in copyright law because, unlike other primary works, their connection to particular forms of entrepreneurial copyright work is less clear. This may be related to a unique feature of many forms of visual art, which is that the original is distinct from, and differently valued, to copies made of it.

Despite all this, there is an understandable tendency in copyright law to treat works of visual art with the same broad brush as other works of primary creativity. Overall, it often appears that when the treatment of works of visual art is compared with the treatment of literary, dramatic and (even) musical works, copyright law makes the simultaneous errors of treating the similar dissimilarly and the dissimilar similarly. Of these two

2. For a discussion of this proposition, see W van Caenegem, 'Copyright, Communication and New Technologies' (1995) 23 *Federal Law Review* 322.

errors, however, that of treating the dissimilar similarly is far more marked. As this paper attempts to show, the particular significance of the anomalous nature of the copyright protection of artistic works lies in its adverse impact on the relationship between the copyright protection of artistic works and artistic practice.

DEFINING ARTISTIC WORKS

The discussion in this paper of the meaning of 'artistic works' for copyright purposes is based upon the definition provided in the United Kingdom Copyright Designs and Patents Act 1988. This definition may be regarded as representative of approaches prevalent in common law jurisdictions.[3] It is found in section 4, which provides as follows:

(1) In this Part 'artistic work' means –
   (a) a graphic work, photograph, sculpture or collage, irrespective of artistic quality,
   (b) a work of architecture being a building or a model for a building, or
   (c) a work of artistic craftsmanship.

(2) In this Part –
'building' includes any fixed structure, and a part of a building or fixed structure;
'graphic work' includes –
   (a) any painting, drawing, diagram, map, chart or plan, and
   (b) any engraving, etching, lithograph, woodcut or similar work;

'photograph' means a recording of light or other radiation on any medium on which an image is produced or from which an image may by any means be produced, and which is not part of a film;

3. See, eg, the Australian Copyright Act 1968, s 10(1), in which the definition of 'artistic work' is very similar.

'sculpture' includes a cast or model made for the purposes of sculpture.

There are three interrelated aspects of this definition upon which this paper will focus. First, the fact that the creation of a list, even a rather ragbag list of this sort, immediately has an exclusionary effect. Secondly, the paper will consider the problematic reference to 'artistic quality', which is said to be irrelevant to those things mentioned in subsection (1)(a), while no such limitation is made in relation to works of architecture or works of artistic craftsmanship. This creates a contentious relationship between the copyright protection of artistic works and notions of 'art' and 'artistic quality'. Thirdly, the paper will examine the peculiarity of putting all these different things together under the generic heading of 'artistic works' and thus treating them as though they were in some way related or similar.

(A) The Exclusionary Effect of the List

Despite the wide appreciation of the fact that there are many different types of literary, dramatic and musical works, it is fairly standard for copyright statutes to give little explanation of the meaning of 'literary', 'dramatic' and 'musical'.[4] Things are rather different in relation to the category of artistic works. In the case of the UK copyright legislation, the list of artistic works now appearing in section 4 is the product of gradual accretion, beginning with the protection of engravings in 1735.[5] It appears that little regard has been given to the relationship of the listed

4. See, eg, the UK Copyright Designs and Patents Act 1988, s 3(1).
5. Engraving Copyright Act of 1734. This was followed by the protection of calico designs in 1787; sculptures in 1798 (Sculpture Copyright Act of 1798 as amended in 1814); prints & lithographs in 1852 (International Copyright Act of 1852); drawings, paintings and photographs in 1862 (Fine Art Copyright Act of 1862); works of artistic craftsmanship in 1911 (Copyright Act of 1911); & collages in 1988 (Copyright Designs & Patents Act 1988): L Bently & B Sherman, *Intellectual Property Law* (Oxford: Oxford University Press, 2001), 62 & 62n; S Stokes, *Art & Copyright* (Oxford: Hart Publishing, 2001), 23-25.

items with each other, especially the extent to which the various things may overlap with each other.[6]

More significantly, the creation of a list is by its nature exclusionary and constricts the flexibility of the law to adapt to new forms of artistic practice. A good example of this occurred in the *Oasis* case.[7] This case concerned the assemblage of various objects along with the members of the British band, Oasis, in a swimming pool. The purpose of this assemblage was to create a photograph for the band's upcoming album cover. It was argued that the assemblage itself was an artistic work because it was a sculpture, a work of artistic craftsmanship, and/or a collage. All three characterisations were rejected: sculpture because there was no element of carving or modelling; work of artistic craftsmanship because there was no element of craftsmanship; and collage because, surprisingly, there was no glue or adhesive involved.

As Stokes points out,[8] a particularly interesting part of the judgment of Lloyd J was his consideration of the argument by counsel for the plaintiffs that section 4 ought not to be construed so as to deny copyright protection to new forms of artistic works. Lloyd J considered a range of contemporary art forms that appeared to raise problems of characterisation under section 4, including things such as Gilbert and George's living sculptures, Rachel Whiteread's house, and many forms of installation art. In the end, he did not address the question of whether or not these were 'artistic works' for copyright purposes. He simply decided that the assemblage in the *Oasis* case was ephemeral and, therefore, to be distinguished from these other works. This is a point to which this paper will return. What we may, at least, take from this case is that the arrangement of found objects (*objets trouvés*)

6. Eg, the extent of overlap between sculptures and works of artistic craftsmanship is problematic, especially since sculptures are protected 'irrespective of artistic quality' while no such limitation applies to works of artistic craftsmanship.
7. *Creation Records Ltd v News Group Newspapers Ltd* [1997] EMLR 445.
8. Stokes, n 5 *supra*, 35-36.

or ready-mades[9] is outside copyright protection, unless perhaps they are permanently situated. It may be that all ready-mades, whether assembled or not, are simply outside copyright protection.[10]

Perhaps cases like the *Oasis Case* are as much a tribute to conservatism and the failure of judicial imagination as they are to the exclusionary effect of a list. Either way, however, they raise serious concerns about the relationship between copyright protection and new forms of artistic practice. However, as we are about to see, the difficulty of both legislators and judges in dealing with the concept of 'artistic works' is not limited merely to new forms of artistic practice.

(B) The Significance of Artistic Quality

To someone who is not a copyright expert, the notion that works are artistic works 'irrespective of artistic quality' may be problematic – but this type of oxymoron is not atypical in copyright law. As a consequence, those accustomed to the peculiarities of copyright law bravely face the concepts of the protected literary work with no literary merit and the protected artistic work with no artistic merit. What is alarming, however, about the definition of 'artistic works' in s. 4 is that only those types of artistic works referred to in paragraph (a) are protected irrespective of artistic quality, suggesting that artistic quality or merit may be relevant to works of architecture and works of artistic craftsmanship.

The struggles of the English courts with the notion of 'works of artistic craftsmanship' are well known.[11] What is very clear

9. According to Stokes, n 5 *supra*, 2n, citing Chilvers, *A Dictionary of Twentieth-Century Art* (Oxford: Oxford University Press, 1999), '"[r]eady-made" is the name given by Marcel Duchamp to a type of work he created which consists of mass-produced article isolated for its functional context and displayed as a work of art'.
10. Stokes notes that this would exclude Marcel Duchamp's bicycle wheel attached to a stool, which was exhibited in 1913 with a view to challenging ideas about the nature of art: n 5 *supra*, 124. Cf Bently & Sherman, n 5 *supra*, 63.
11. See, eg, *George Hensher Ltd v Restawile Upholstery (Lancs) Ltd* [1975] RPC 31, *Merlet v Mothercare plc* [1986] RPC 115, *Vermaat v Boncrest Ltd*, *The Times*, 23 June 2000.

from these cases is that despite the absence of the expression 'irrespective of artistic quality' in paragraph (c), which suggests that artistic quality is relevant, the courts have declined to be drawn into the question of whether or not the work of artistic craftsmanship has artistic merit. Rather they have considered issues such as the aim and impact of the craftsman/creator[12] and the motivations of those wishing to acquire the work in question.[13] Arguably what they are considering in these cases is whether or not the work has the quality or nature of an artistic work, not whether it has artistic quality or merit. It is clearly the case that judges have undertaken this same enquiry in relation to artistic works falling within paragraph (a). That is, they have enquired whether or not the work has the quality or nature of an artistic work of the type in question. Arguably, exactly this sort of consideration lay behind the decision of Laddie J in *Metix (UK) Ltd v G H Maughan (Plastics) Ltd*.[14] In this case Laddie J held that a sculpture was 'a three dimensional work made by an artist's hand' and that, consequently, casts used for making double-barrelled cartridge syringes were not sculptures because they could not be regarded as the work of an artist.[15] Another rather less overt example of the court enquiring into whether a work has the nature or quality of the type of artistic work in question occurred in the *Adam Ant* case.[16] Faced with the argument that the make-up on Adam's face was a graphic work in the form of a painting, Lawton LJ said a painting 'is not an idea: it is an object' and as such it must be affixed to a surface.[17] Thus suggesting the notion that one of the qualities of a painting, if not artistic works more generally, is permanent fixation. There is no obvious reason why a painting or a work of art must be permanently affixed and it is argued below that the result of such a

12. See *Hensher v Restawile*, n 11 *supra*, per Lord Simon of Glaisdale; & *Merlet v Mothercare*, n 11 *supra*.
13. See *Hensher v Restawile*, n 11 *supra*, per Lord Reid & Lord Simon of Glaisdale.
14. [1997] FSR 719.
15. Cf *Hi-Tech Autoparts Ltd v Towergate Two Limited* [2002] FSR 15, in which the court refused to extend this reasoning to graphic works.
16. *Merchandising v Harpbond* [1983] FSR 32.
17. *Ibid.*, 46.

determination is to exclude particular types of visual art from the protection of copyright law.

(C) TREATING THE DISSIMILAR SIMILARLY I: THE PERMANENCE REQUIREMENT

In relation to the copyright definition of an 'artistic work', one of the primary manifestations of the phenomenon whereby the dissimilar is treated similarly is the requirement of permanent affixation derived from the *Adam Ant* case. As discussed above, in this case Lawton LJ held that facial make-up was not a painting as it was not permanently affixed to a surface. Even as a dictum on the definition of a painting for the purpose of the copyright definition of artistic works, this is problematic enough in terms of the relationship between copyright law and artistic practice. There has, however, been considerable confusion about how widely this troublesome dictum applies. That is, does it apply just to paintings, just to graphic works, just to works falling within the first paragraph of the definition of artistic works, or to all artistic works? It is clear that the more widely one applies this rule, the more limiting its effects become. If it applies only to paintings or other graphic works, it might exclude, for example, impermanent chalk drawings. If applied more widely, the concept of permanence might exclude from the definition of artistic works things like sand sculptures, ice sculptures and much installation art. Despite this (or perhaps because of it), the general trend in judicial approaches in common law countries has been to read the requirement widely. So, for example, in the *Oasis* case,[18] one of the reasons why the collection of *objet trouvés* was held not to be a sculpture, collage or work of artistic craftsmanship was that it was not intended to remain permanently in its particular arrangement. In the Australian case of *Komesaroff v Mickle*[19] the requirement of permanence was extended to the category of works of artistic craftsmanship with the result that so-called sand pictures, the contents of which move and change appearance depending upon the angle at which the picture is

18. Note 7 *supra*.
19. [1988] RPC 204.

placed, did not qualify as artistic works. However, just to complicate the situation, contemporaneously with the *Oasis* case, the UK case of *Metix v Maughan*[20] questioned the requirement of permanence in relation to, at least, sculptures. Laddie J noted that such a requirement would, for example, exclude ice sculptures.

One might argue that the somewhat uncertain state of the law with respect to the application of the permanence requirement is the inevitable result of taking a characteristic that may possibly apply to one form of artistic work and attempting to extend it through the whole diverse category of artistic works. The discomfort of Laddie J in *Metix* with the idea that ice sculptures might be excluded from copyright protection may demonstrate a laudable awareness of the consequences of the over-extension of the permanence requirement. Generally, however, it is arguable that the more common discomfort that members of the judiciary feel in relation to the whole category of artistic works has resulted in the misapplication of an inappropriate but comprehensible rule. The tendency to extend such a rule to such a range of different forms of artistic expression is clearly encouraged by the lumping together of widely diverse forms of artistic creativity under one generic heading of 'artistic works'.

Striking the Copyright Balance

A major theme of copyright law lies in striking the appropriate balance between the protection of creativity and the stimulation of further forms of creativity. This is a notoriously difficult task in relation to all types of creativity protected by copyright law. It is nevertheless essential that copyright law recognise that the creative process draws upon the influence of earlier works[21] with

20. Note 14 *supra*.
21. In relation to the influence of earlier music on later musical works, see S Vaidhyanathan, *Copyrights & Copywrongs: The Rise of Intellectual Property & How it Threatens Creativity* (New York: New York University Press, 2001),ch 4. See generally, F Macmillan Patfield, 'Towards a Reconciliation of Free

the result that overprotection of those works will stifle creativity. In the context of actions for infringement of copyright, the main tools for achieving this balance are said to be the idea/expression dichotomy and the fair dealing defences to an action for infringement. It is arguable, however, that in relation to artistic works these concepts have failed to achieve the necessary balance. The discussion below posits three related reasons for this. First is the fact that idiosyncratic copyright rules on infringement in relation to artistic works unnecessarily lower the threshold for copyright infringement. Secondly, particular difficulties have been encountered in applying the idea/expression dichotomy in relation to artistic works. Thirdly, much modern artistic practice specifically seeks to challenge the propertisation of artistic works through copyright law and its neighbouring law of moral rights.

(A) TREATING THE DISSIMILAR SIMILARLY II: SHAPE SHIFTING

If the permanence requirement was the only example of the dangers of grouping together dissimilar things as though they were essentially similar, the argument that this was a matter of concern might ring rather hollow. It seems, however, that the permanence requirement is only one example of a mindset in copyright law that is seriously out of kilter with the reality of artistic practice. Another pertinent example of the tendency to treat the dissimilar similarly in relation to artistic works arises in relation to the particular rules governing the infringement of copyright in artistic works. In most common law jurisdictions there is a statutory provision to the effect that the reproduction of a two-dimensional artistic work in three dimensions, or the reproduction of a three-dimensional work in two dimensions, constitutes an infringement of the work.[22] This rule only applies to the infringement of artistic works so that, for example, the three-dimensional reproduction of a literary work (such as the

Speech and Copyright' in E Barendt (ed), *The Yearbook of Media and Entertainment Law 1996* (1996) 199.

22. See, eg, the UK Copyright Designs and Patents Act 1988, s 17(3).

knitting of a jumper in accordance with a written knitting pattern) is not an infringement. The exclusivity of this rule immediately raises problems in relation to works that seek to challenge the boundaries between artistic works and other types of copyright works.[23] However, even in the context of works that recognisably fall within the copyright definition of artistic works, this rule is problematic.

This two dimensional/three dimensional rule was, of course, at the heart of the famous (or infamous) case of *Rogers v Koons*,[24] in which Jeff Koons was found to have infringed copyright when he created a sculpture based upon a well-known photo by Art Rogers of a couple holding seven puppies. Koons' sculpture, 'String of Puppies', which was produced for the purpose of his exhibition, 'The Banality Show', was anything but a close copy in three dimensions. In both intention and effect the sculpture was a parody of the photograph. This case is ordinarily seen as raising serious issues about the utility of fair dealing/fair use defence,[25] upon which some comment is made below. However, it is also worth noting that there would not have been an infringement in the first place, but for the two dimensional/three dimensional rule. The visual artist JSG Boggs has noted that the result in this case demonstrates that copyright law fails to understand that sculpture and photography are quite distinct disciplines. As a result, a sculpture can no more be reasonably regarded as a copy of a photograph than can a written description of that photograph.[26] However, copyright law has created a false commonality or similarity between different artistic disciplines that allows results that appear meaningless to practitioners of

23. This is a persistent trend in modern artistic practice. For more on works that seek to erase the distinction between art and literature, see A Julius, *Transgressions: The Offences of Art* (New York: Thames & Hudson, 2002), 122.
24. 751 F Supp 474 (SDNY 1990), aff'd 960 F 2d 301 (2d Cir), cert denied, 113 S Ct 365 (1992).
25. See, eg, W Landes, 'Copyright, borrowed images and appropriation art: an economic approach ' in R Towse (ed), *Copyright in the Cultural Industries* (London: Edward Elgar Publisher, 2002) 9, 24-25
26. JSG Boggs, 'Who Owns This?' (1993) 68 *Chicago-Kent Law Review* 889, 898-900.

art. What is more, if this is correct, these sorts of results cast serious doubt over the role of the idea/expression dichotomy in relation to artistic works.

(B) Treating the Dissimilar Similarly III: Idea and Expression

Famously, the idea/expression dichotomy provides that copyright protects, not the idea underlying the work, but rather its expression.[27] How can the notion that copyright protects the expression of an idea rather than the idea itself be maintained when the two dimensional/three dimensional infringement rule means that copyright is protecting a completely dissimilar expression of the idea in question? That is, where it is protecting an expression that is as dissimilar to the copyright work as is a written description of the content of a photograph.[28] It is, of course, the case that to make an adaptation of a literary, dramatic or musical work is to infringe copyright in that work,[29] but the concept of adaptation does not catch works that are fundamentally dissimilar to the copyright work in question. Adaptations of literary works, for example, are still literary works.

It is clear that cases like *Rogers v Koons* show the two-dimensional/three-dimensional rule in its worst light. There may be other cases in which the making of a two-dimensional copy of a three-dimensional work (and vice versa) involves the making of a close copy and the consequent unjustifiable and non-creative exploitation of another's work. This suggests that a significant part of the problem here is the failure to make the application of the two-dimensional/three-dimensional infringement rule subject to the overriding principle that an infringement only takes place where the copier takes the whole or a substantial part[30] of the expression, not the idea, of the work. Depressingly, however,

27. See, eg, *Donoghue v Allied Newspapers* [1938] Ch 106; *Ravenscroft v Herbert* [1980] RPC 193; *Fraser v Thames Television* [1983] 2 All ER 101; *Green v Broadcasting Corporation* [1989] RPC 469 & 700 (PC).
28. See text acc n 26 *supra*.
29. See, eg, the UK Copyright Designs and Patents Act 1988, ss 16(1)(e) & 21.
30. See, eg, UK Copyright Designs and Patents Act 1988, s 16(3)(a).

a review of the judicial application of the idea/expression dichotomy in the context of artistic works does not suggest that it would do much to ameliorate the excesses of the two-dimensional/three-dimensional infringement rule.

In general, the notion that an idea can be divorced from its expression is not an easy one to embrace, except at the most banal level. The reason for this is that the way an idea is expressed is part of the idea itself.[31] This is particularly so in relation to a wide range of artistic works and it means that even fatuous examples are difficult. We might say that the fact that one person paints a particular scene does not prevent someone else also painting it, but we would say it with some caution in the UK after a case such as *Krisarts v Briarfine*.[32] In this case, which was an interlocutory judgment, the defendants used paintings of certain views in London as one of the influences in creating their own paintings of the same scenes. The defendants' paintings were not particularly similar to the paintings in which the plaintiffs owned copyright; nevertheless the court held that an arguable case of copyright infringement existed.

As already noted, consideration of the idea/expression dichotomy in copyright cases is closely associated with the question of whether or not the defendant has copied a substantial part of the plaintiff's copyright work. A UK case that considered this matter in relation to artistic works is the House of Lords decision in *Designer Guild Ltd v Russell Williams (Textiles) Ltd.*[33] This case concerned fabric designs. The plaintiff's design, 'Ixia' was based on a painting by one of its employees. Said to be inspired by the 'handwriting and feel' of Matisse, the plaintiff's painting and consequent fabric design was constituted by stripes overlaid by impressionistically scattered flowers. The defendant's design, 'Marguerite' also had stripes and impressionistically scattered flowers. The plaintiff argued that the defendant's design copied a substantial part of his 'Ixia' design and, consequently, constituted an indirect copying of the original painting of the design.

31. For an elaboration of this argument, see Macmillan Patfield, n 21 *supra*, 216-219.
32. [1977] FSR 577.
33. [2000] 1 WLR 2416 (HL).

The Court of Appeal took the view that 'Marguerite' did not copy a substantial part of the expression of the idea of 'Ixia'. That is, even though the elements (stripes and flowers) were similar and the means of executing the ideas were similar (similar brushwork and resist effect), the overall 'visual effect' was different.[34] The House of Lords unanimously rejected the approach of the Court of Appeal and found, like the original trial judge, that an infringement had taken place. All the members of the House of Lords considered the question of whether or not substantial taking had occurred. Lord Hoffman specifically considered this in relation to the idea/expression dichotomy. He took the view that different ideas expressed in the copyright work can be abstracted from the whole and thus form a substantial part, which if annexed by someone else, will result in an infringement. Thus, the stripes and flowers together form a substantial part of the work with the result that when they are used without authorisation an infringement occurs. The end result in this case was that, despite the fact that the defendant's 'Marguerite' design is not all that visually similar to the plaintiff's 'Ixia' design, an infringement was said to have occurred.

When judges struggle with the meaning of words and expressions like 'artistic' and 'artistic quality', when they lay down arbitrary rules about what constitutes a painting or an artistic work, when they struggle with the idea/expression dichotomy and concepts of substantial taking in relation to artistic works, what they may be demonstrating is a particular discomfort with the nature of creativity in the visual arts. Where these struggles result in a decision that copyright is infringed by a piece of visual art that is visually dissimilar to another work, then copyright law may start to have a serious impact on the way in which visual artists exercise their creativity. Further, such unequal struggles inspire little confidence in copyright law's ability to deal with artistic practices that challenge the very concepts of copyright law.

34. [2000] FSR 121 (CA), 134 per Morritt LJ.

(C) CHALLENGING COPYRIGHT

The postmodern practice[35] of appropriation art in which a familiar image is relocated and recontextualised in a new work of visual art is well exemplified by Jeff Koons' use of Art Rogers' photograph. Appropriation art might, itself, be relocated within the wider context of subversive or transgressive art, involving what Julius has described as 'art crimes':

> Though art crimes are a constant in the history of art-making it is only in the modern period that the committing of art crimes against art works becomes an aesthetic project, and criminal artworks, objects of aesthetic interest. There are two types of these art crimes: offences of reproduction and offences of destruction.
>
> Offences of reproduction are at or near the terminal point of a notional arc that begins with an original work, and then travels through pastiche, plagiarism, breach of copyright, misattribution of authorship and passing off, to forgery. Offences of destruction are at the terminal point of an arc that begins with an original work, and then travels through adaptations, then parody, then breach of moral rights, trespass, suppression or other breach of speech rights, to criminal damage.[36]

Both types of 'art crimes' involve challenges to a wide range of copyright concepts. Some of these challenges are illustrated by a consideration of subversive or transgressive art practices in the context of the law on fair dealing/fair use and moral rights.[37]

Hutcheon has noted that '[r]eappropriating existing representations that are effective precisely because they are loaded

35. It may be argued that this practice has its roots in Dadaism, Surrealism and Pop Art: see B Sherman, 'Appropriating the Postmodern: Copyright and the Challenge of the New' in D McLean & K Schubert (eds), *Dear Images: Art, Copyright and Culture* (London: Institute of Contemporary Arts & Ridinghouse, 2002) 405, 405 citing A Bonnett, 'Art, ideology and everyday space: subversive tendencies from Dada to postmodernism' (1992) 10 *Society and Space* 69. See also, Stokes, n 5 *supra*, 125 & 125n.
36. Julius, n 23 *supra*, 87.
37. These are not, of course, the only copyright concepts challenged by postmodern art practices. Particular challenges are also made to the concepts of originality and authorship: see K Bowrey, 'Copyright, the Paternity of Artistic Works and the Challenge Posed by Postmodern Artists' (1994) 8 *Intellectual Property Journal* 285. See also, A Wilson, ''This is Not by Me'. Andy Warhol and the Question of Authorship' in McClean & Schubert, n 36 *supra*, 375.

with pre-existing meaning and putting them into new and ironic contexts is a typical form of postmodern ... critique'.[38] Consistently with this approach, in *Rogers v Koons*, Koons argued that he was entitled to the protection of the fair use doctrine on the basis that his work was a parody for the purpose of criticizing the banality of popular cultural images. The US Supreme Court held, however, that the fair use defence only applies where the infringing work has used a copyright work for the purpose of criticising that copyright work, rather than for the purpose of criticising society in general. This suggests that the fair use defence will avail appropriation artists in only a very limited range of cases. Julius has identified transgressive art as falling within three general groups: art that questions the meaning or methods of art; art that breaks taboos; and, art that has a political motivation.[39] If the fair use/fair dealing defence protects only a critique of a particular work of art, it seems unlikely that it will offer much protection to transgressive forms of appropriation art. In particular, appropriation art that breaks taboos or has a political motivation appears to be outside the protection of the fair use/fair dealing defence. Optimists may argue that subsequent decisions on both sides of the Atlantic in cases like *Campbell v Acuff-Rose Music, Inc*[40] and *Time Warner Entertainments Company LP v Channel 4 Television Corporation plc*[41] repair or mitigate some of the damage that *Rogers v Koons* has done to the vitality of the fair dealing/fair use defence. It is true that *Time Warner*, in particular, would appear to permit the use of the fair dealing defence for the purpose of making a wider social comment. However, not only has this mish-mash of case law created confusion about the scope of the defence, there is some concern in the UK context that even a more generous application of the fair

38. L Hutcheon, *The Politics of Postmodernism* (London: Routledge, 1989), 44. This passage is also quoted in Stokes, n 5 *supra*, 125n.
39. Julius, n 23 *supra*, ch III.
40. 114 S Ct 1164 (1994). For a fuller discussion of this case in the context of the relationship between copyright & free speech, see Macmillan Patfield, n 21 *supra*, 226-230.
41. [1994] EMLR 1. For a fuller discussion of this case in the context of the relationship between copyright & free speech, see Macmillan Patfield, n 21 *supra*, 226-230.

dealing defence than that allowed in *Rogers v Koons* might be undermined by a robust application of the original artist's moral rights.

Two aspects of moral rights law are in the frame here. The first is the copyright author's right of integrity[42] and the second is the right against false attribution.[43] In relation to the right of integrity, the right to object to a distortion of a copyright work seems to have a somewhat fatal effect on exactly the type of appropriation for the purposes of pastiche or parody that *Rogers v Koons* suggests would fall within the protection of the fair use defence. That is, an appropriation for the purposes of parody or pastiche that has the intention or effect of criticising the copyright work may very well be deemed a distortion of the work prejudicial to the honour or reputation of the author. There is some basis for arguing that some parodic appropriations for the purpose of making a social comment, rather than commenting on the appropriated work, would fare better under moral rights law. The Swedish case of *Svanberg v Eriksson*[44] considered the exhibition of a reproduction of an artistic work to which printed comments and printing instructions had been added for the purposes of making a comment on the commercial exploitation of graphic art. This was not regarded as a breach of the original artist's right of integrity as there was no material alteration to the central elements of the work.[45] On the other hand, one might have thought that the sort of distortion involved in a case like *Rogers v Koons* would raise an arguable case of a breach of the right of integrity. It is interesting to note, however, that the distortions in both *Svanberg v Eriksson* and *Rogers v Koons* were not to the original artwork.[46] There are some grounds, examined below, for supposing that the courts will only find a breach of the right of integrity where the original work is distorted. If this is correct then this may pose some problems for some types

42. UK Copyright, Designs and Patents Act 1988, s 80.
43. UK Copyright, Designs and Patents Act 1988, s 84.
44. [1979] *European Intellectual Property Review* D-93.
45. See further Stokes, n 5 *supra*, 137.
46. Whatever that might be considered to be in the case of a photograph.

of transgressive art, but would seem to leave appropriation art largely unscathed by the right of integrity.

So far as breaches of moral rights in relation to appropriation art are concerned, it only remains to note that the recontextualisation of the appropriated image might raise the possibility of a breach of the right against false attribution. It seems likely, however, that this right will only be infringed where the paternity of the appropriation artist is not clear.[47]

The Significance of the Original

The materiality of visual art echoes through much of the above discussion. The apparently philistine epigram of Lawton LJ in the *Adam Ant* case that a painting 'is not an idea: it is an object'[48] may have been (subconsciously) influenced by the materiality issue. Perhaps Lawton LJ meant what Teilmann has said much more elegantly: 'Visual art is not separable from its materiality, from the physical entity of the painting, or the drawing, or the sculpture. Texts on the contrary are characteristically immaterial'.[49] Similarly, when Boggs expresses incredulity at the idea that a sculpture can constitute a copy of a photograph,[50] perhaps he is partly getting at the same sort of thing as Kant who suggests that to make, for example, an engraving of a painting is not to make a copy of it because the painting is a unique object, which cannot be copied by an engraving.[51] As Teilmann has noted, Kant is also making the point that some types of artistic works are not susceptible to the dangers of copying in the same

47. See *Clark v Associated Newspapers Ltd* [1998] 1 All ER 959. See further, M Blakeney & F Macmillan, 'Journalistic Parody and Moral Rights under Australian Copyright Law' (1998) 3 *Media & Arts Law Review* 124.
48. See n 17 *supra*, & accompanying text.
49. S Teilmann 'Framing the Law: Authorship of Images', Paper presented at the *Crossroads in Cultural Studies Conference*, Tampere, Finland, June 2002. See also S Teilmann 'Framing the Law: The Right of Integrity in Britain' [2005] 27 EIPR 19.
50. See n 26 *supra*, and & accompanying text.
51. See Teilmann, n 49 *supra*, citing Kant, 'Von der Unrechtmäßigkeit der Büchernachdrucks', *Berlinische Monatsschrift* 5 (May 1785), 403-417.

ways that others are because the original will always be more valued and valuable than any copy.[52]

The materiality of some types of visual arts contrasts, especially these days, with literary works, which are immaterial.[53] The first manuscript is a step in the process of the expression of the idea to the public rather than an end in itself. In terms of the expression of the literary work, one copy of a book is as good as another. On the other hand, a painting or sculpture, for example, cannot be separated from its own materiality and is, therefore, an end in itself rather than merely a means to an end.[54] Of course, there are a number of types of artistic works protected by copyright law that lack the characteristic of materiality. This would be true, for example, of technical drawings, which fall within the definition of drawing and thus within the definition of a graphic work.[55] It is true of many photographs. It is also true of some things categorised by copyright law as sculptures.[56] This distinction between material and immaterial works seems to go to the heart of copyright law, which is after all a right to prevent copying. The meaningfulness and operation of such a right must surely be qualitatively different for material and immaterial works.[57] If this is so then for copyright law to be relevant to artistic practice the protection that artists need from both copyright law and its neighbouring moral rights law may be different depending upon whether or not they are creating works intended to be unique one-off pieces or whether they are creating works that are purely for the purposes of reproduction.

52. Teilmann, n 49 *supra*.
53. *Ibid*.
54. Teilmann, n 49 *supra*.
55. See, eg, UK Copyright, Designs and Patents Act 1988, s 4(2); & see *Solar Thompson v Barton* [1977] RPC 537.
56. See, eg, *Wham-O Manufacturing Co v Lincoln Industries Ltd* [1985] RPC 127; & *Breville Europe plc v Thorn EMI Domestic Appliances Ltd* [1995] FSR 77.
57. In fact, the very idea presents a challenge to notions of intellectual property, which is usually characterised as non-rivalrous and non-crowdable: see, eg, J Waldron, 'From Authors to Copiers: Individual Rights & Social Values in Intellectual Property' (1993) 69 *Chicago-Kent Law Review* 841, 870-874.

It might be argued that as a right against copying, copyright is irrelevant to works of visual art in which the value resides in the original one-off work. On the other hand, it is also arguable that the creators of such works are entitled to protection from unauthorised commercialisation of such works in the form of, for example, photographs. At the least copyright law needs to find a mechanism for treating the copyright owners of unique one-off pieces like other copyright owners by giving them a financial stake in the work based on the demand for the work in the marketplace. For other copyright owners that demand will be reflected in the demand for reproductions. For the copyright owner of the unique one-off artistic work, the demand for such work in the market place is largely reflected in the price put on the one-off item.[58] This might be reflected in the introduction of a resale right for the copyright holder. To be consistent with the general tenor of copyright law this economic right should belong to the copyright holder, not to the artist-author, in order to put the copyright holder of a one-off artistic work in an economic position that reflects the economic position of other copyright holders. The artist will, of course, be the beneficiary of this, provided he or she retains copyright in their work. The economic loss suffered by the artist who transfers his or her copyright along with the physical ownership of the item is, in many ways, no different to any other author of a copyright work who transfers away their copyright only to find that the work subsequently becomes much more valuable. It is interesting that the *droit de suite*, which exists in most EU countries, confers a resale right on the artist, not on the copyright holder. This is not surprising given the (obvious) origins of the *droit de suite* in a *droit d'auteur* system.[59] Resistance to the *droit de suite* in Anglo-American copyright systems may owe something to the fact that,

58. If a painting or sculpture becomes particularly famous there may be a demand for reproductions of the painting on postcards, in books and so on. However, the return on such demand will ordinarily be a poor reflection of the increase in value of the original item.
59. On the differences between the *droit d'auteur* system and the Anglo-American conception of copyright, see generally JAL Sterling, *World Copyright Law* (London: Sweet & Maxwell, 2003).

unlike the usual tenor of copyright law in such systems, it gives to the author rather than to the copyright owner the benefit of any increase in the market value of the work. To date, the result of this resistance has been that in the world's largest art markets[60] neither the copyright owner nor the artist-author benefits from increases in the market value of a one-off work of visual art unless either of them also happens to be the owner of the physical property in the art work.

So far as the moral rights of the author of a one-off work are concerned there is some basis upon which to suspect that judges implicitly take into account the distinction between works that are intended to be an end in themselves and works that are intended or designed to be exactly reproducible. In making this argument, Teilmann[61] cites the UK cases of *Tidy v Trustees of the Natural History Museum*[62] and *Pasterfield v Denham*[63] concerning the moral right of integrity.[64] In both of these cases the distortions to which the artists objected were reproductions of the work, rather than to the originals. The courts declined to follow the Canadian case of *Snow v The Eaton Centre Ltd*,[65] in which the distortion occurred to the original work. Teilmann suggests 'cautiously' that there may be significance in the fact that the English cases concerned treatment of the reproductions while the Canadian case concerned the original and unique work. This suggestion is also consistent with the outcome, if not the dicta, of *Svanberg v Eriksson*.[66] If the suggestion is correct, then it may be that

60. New York and London. In 2000 it was estimated that the UK controls 70% of the European Union art market: see Stokes, n 5 *supra*, 80. On the *droit de suite*, see generally Stokes, n 5 *supra*, 76-86.
61. Note 49 *supra*.
62. [1998] 39 IPR 501.
63. [1999] 26 FSR 168.
64. See the UK Copyright Designs and Patents Act 1988, s 80.
65. 70 CPR (2d) 105 (1982), in which it was held that a breach of the author's right of integrity occurred when a shopping centre altered the appearance of a sculpture depicting Canadian geese in their migratory pattern by tying putatively festive red and green ribbons around the necks of the geese.
66. See nn 44-46 *supra*, & acc text. The Supreme Court of Sweden appeared to accept that a breach of the right of integrity might have occurred as a result of a distortion of a copy of the work.

this distinction between works that are an end in themselves and other copyright works is being recognised in a way that prejudices the artists of one-off works. On the other hand, it may also be responsible for ensuring that the right of integrity in relation to artistic works does not undermine possible gains for artistic practice arising from the fair dealing/fair use defence.[67]

It seems rather unsatisfactory that the possible clash between the fair dealing/fair use rights and the right of integrity of authors can be solved in the case of one-off artistic works, but not other copyright works, by taking away the moral right of the artist to exercise any control over the treatment of copies of the work.[68] In general, a more coherent resolution of the tension between the concepts of fair dealing and the right of integrity is necessary. More specifically, the law of copyright and neighbouring rights needs to give attention to the question of the applicability of its general concepts to works that are unique one-off pieces, copies of which will always be qualitatively different from the original. If the logical conclusion of such a consideration is to deny to the authors of such works the protection of the right of integrity in relation to copies, then the corollary of this must be that authors of such works are entitled to a moral right to prevent the destruction of the unique original physical object in which their creativity is embedded.[69] It is not impossible that the right of integrity in fact gives this protection, but it not clear. Giving such protection will, of course, impact upon the type of transgressive art that involves the destruction of original art works.[70] However, such work is of such an order of conscious transgression that any inhibition provided by a moral right against destruction of an original art work would be likely to be

67. See text acc nn 42-46 *supra*.

68. At least in the case of some types of artistic work, it also seems inconsistent with the provisions of, eg, the UK Copyright Designs and Patents Act 1988, s 80(4).

69. See also Teilmann, n 49 *supra*, who cites as an example of such an approach the right to 'protection against destruction' in Article 15(1) of the Swiss Federal Law on Copyright of 9 October 1992, as amended.

70. See, eg, Julius, n 26 *supra*, 87, & text acc n 36 *supra*.

balanced by the stimulating effect of transgressing not only artistic convention, but also moral rights as defined by law.

Artistic Practice and the Rationales for Copyright: Some Tentative Conclusions

The role and purpose of copyright law is a matter of considerable academic debate.[71] A number of dominant themes in relation to the justification and rationalisation of copyright law have emerged from this debate. These include, most notably, economic or utilitarian justifications, natural right justifications, and personality right justifications. Economic or utilitarian justifications posit that copyright provides an economic incentive to creators and exploiters of copyright work, thus encouraging the creation and dissemination of cultural works with consequent cultural development.[72] Natural rights justifications are said to spring from Lockean theories of property[73] and involve the proposition that the author is entitled to a reward for the creation of the work in question. Personality right justifications, generally attributed to the writings of Hegel and Kant,[74] are based on the argument that a work is the embodiment of the personality of the creator and, therefore, should be subject to the creator's

71. For some varied examples of this debate, see W Gordon, 'A Property Right in Self-Expression: Equality & Individualism in the Natural Law of Intellectual Property' (1993) 102 *Yale Law Journal* 1533; F Macmillan Patfield, 'Legal Policy and the Limits of Literary Copyright' in P Parrinder, W Chernaik & W Gould, (eds), *Textual Monopolies: Literary Copyright and the Public Domain* (London: University of London, 1997), 113; J Smiers, 'The Abolition of Copyrights: Better for Artists, Third World Countries and the Public Domain' in R Towse, n 25 *supra*, 120; M Spence, 'Justifying Copyright' in McClean & Schubert, n 36 *supra*, 388; Towse, n 1 *supra*; & Waldron, n 57 *supra*.
72. A famous embrace of this justification may be found in the Preface to the World Intellectual Property Organisation, *Guide to the Berne Convention for the Protection of Literary and Artistic Works* (WIPO Publication No 615(E), 1978).
73. See P Drahos, *A Philosophy of Intellectual Property* (Dartmouth, 1996), ch 3; & Gordon, n 71 *supra*.
74. See Drahos, n 73 *supra*, ch 4; cf Spence, n 71 *supra*, 399.

ownership and/or control. Personality right justifications seem to be particularly important in relation to moral rights. The point of these concluding remarks is not to enter into the general debate about the validity of these rationales, but rather to argue that the confusion and inconsistency of the law on the copyright protection of artistic works raises questions about the efficacy of each of these justifications in relation to the protection of works of visual art. This, in turn, must raise questions about the general efficacy of copyright law in this area.

Reflecting the triadic nature of the discussion in this paper, there are three comments that might be made upon the way in which the copyright protection of artistic works impacts on the dominant rationales for copyright protection. The first of these is that the exclusion of new forms of artistic works from copyright protection – either through exclusion from the list of protected 'artistic works' or through the imposition of meaningless limitations on the content of that list – means that copyright is playing no role in encouraging new forms of artistic practice. In particular, copyright is not providing an incentive for art that questions the meaning of art or art that questions the methods of art. Since this has been the method by which art practice has developed and changed, copyright is playing no cultural development role in this field.

Secondly, the failure to strike the copyright balance appropriately and coherently – as a result of the two-dimensional/three-dimensional infringement rule, the blurring of the idea expression dichotomy, or the confused application of the fair dealing/fair use defences and the moral right of integrity – makes a serious impact on artistic creativity. The character of all types of creativity, including artistic creativity, is to develop, reflect upon and challenge what has gone before.[75] Copyright law needs to tread a fine line between protecting creators from slavish copying, while allowing the development of creative forerunner. If, instead, it allows the unwarranted extension of the

75. It is worth pausing to note in this respect that the 'Ixia' design, which was protected in *Designer Guild Ltd v Russell Williams Textiles (UK) Ltd*, n 33 *supra*, was said to have been inspired by the 'handwriting and feel' of Matisse.

copyright monopoly it will act as a disincentive to creative activity[76] (which is more serious than merely failing to act as an incentive). Thus, through the unwarranted extension of economic and personality rights, it will undermine its own cultural development function.

The final comment that might be made about the impact of copyright's approach to protecting artistic works upon the rationales for copyright, relates to its apparent myopia with regard to the materiality of at least some types of works of visual art. There is an appealing irony in the fact that copyright, in its obsession with the intangible right, has failed to notice this all too tangible reality. Nevertheless, by failing to recognise the essential nature of some artistic works as unique, one-off, ends in themselves, copyright law in many jurisdictions has failed to provide economic incentives for the production of such works; it has failed to recognise the natural rights of authors to be adequately rewarded for the creation and value of such works; it has not dealt coherently with the right of integrity in relation to such works; and it has not generally recognised the most important of all personality rights in relation to such works, which is the right to prevent their physical destruction.

When JSG Boggs observed that in copyright law 'the visual arts have not fared as well in societies born of the English aesthetic, where literature is the supreme form of expression',[77] he appears to have had a point.

76. Essentially by subjecting artistic creativity to the risk of litigation and thus making it an expensive or risky activity: see W Landes & R Posner, 'An Economic Analysis of Copyright Law' (1989) 18 *Journal of Legal Studies* 325.
77. Boggs, n 26 *supra*, 905.

Lawyers and Experts in Danish Copyright Infringement Cases

*Morten Rosenmeier**

Judges are experts in law; they know about the law, court decisions, the constitution, etc. However, there are a number of things that judges do not know about: things they cannot be expected to know anything about. For example, judges cannot be expected to have a precise knowledge of computer science: how computers are constructed, how they work from a technical point of view. Nor can judges be expected to have extensive knowledge of psychology, such as the differences between various psychological theories, the exact views of Freud and Jung and so forth. Neither can one expect a judge to have expert knowledge of, say, medicine, architecture, literature, astronomy and nuclear physics. Judges in Denmark have studied law at university. In other words, they are experts in law.

Even so, judges are frequently confronted with cases where their decision requires specialised knowledge within some field in which they are not experts. Let us take an example: in a dispute over custody of a child the law stipulates that the judge is to base his decision on what is best for the child. The judge can only make his decision if he has access to detailed knowledge of the psychology of the individual family members: of the mother's childhood; of the father's childhood: whether it will be best for the child to live with the mother or the father from a

* Ph.D., Associate Professor of Law, University of Copenhagen

purely psychological point of view. In a word, the judge – the legal expert – is expected to make a decision which requires *psychological expertise.* We shall consider another example: A factory has bought a very advanced, digitally controlled machine from another factory. It turns out that the machine is dysfunctional. Factory no. 1 therefore demands a compensation of 5.000.000 D.kr. from factory no. 2. The relevant part of the law prescribes that the judge must base his decision on whether the machine is faulty or not. This is possible only to the extent that he knows exactly how it works. Thus the judge has to make a decision on the basis of *technical expertise.*

A final example: In a copyright case a designer has created a small wheel intended to go under office chairs. The creator thinks his wheel exceptionally nice, in fact to be considered a little artistic work eligible for copyright protection. Subsequently a furniture manufacturer initiates production of an office-chair wheel, which greatly resembles the copyright wheel. Although the two wheels are not perfectly identical the designer sues the furniture manufacturer for copyright infringement. A basic rule of copyright law is that to be eligible for copyright protection as an 'artistic work' a thing must be both 'art' and 'original'. Furthermore, a fundamental principle of copyright is there may be infringement even when a work is merely 'substantially similar' to a work in copyright. The judge therefore has to answer three difficult questions before making his decision. Firstly, what is 'art', including the question of whether wheels that are supposed to go under an office chair can be art? Secondly, what does it imply that something is 'original', and when are wheels that are supposed to be put under office chairs original? And thirdly: What degree of similarity between the designer's and the defendant's wheels is required to cause them to be 'substantially similar', involving copyright infringement? Some of these questions – including the question of originality – can only be answered if the judge has precise information about *aesthetic* questions. For instance, the designer's wheels are probably only original if they are different from other wheels on the market. Whether this is the case is in fact a matter for aesthetic judgement. The judge – the expert in law – decides in a case which requires *aesthetic expertise.*

TECHNICAL MATTERS AND LEGAL MATTERS

Situations like these leave the judge a problem to be solved in some way. Danish courts have traditionally solved the question by drawing on one or more experts before the courts make their decisions. In the child custody case where the judge needs psychological knowledge of the parents and their child the court often gets a statement from a psychologist; the psychologist explains to the judge what is best for the child from a psychological point of view. Then the judge makes his decision, based on the psychologist's statement. In the case where the judge has to decide whether a machine is faulty, the parties often get a statement from an engineer, who can evaluate the machine from a technical point of view, and the judge bases his decision on the engineer's expertise. In the example of the copyright case where the judge was to decide if a wheel for an office chair is an original work, the parties invite statements from expert in aesthetics – such as professional designers or architects – as to whether the wheel is original or not. Then the judge makes his decision on the basis of the expert's statement. Danish judges normally attach considerable importance to experts' statements, indeed, in the view of many lawyers, they attach too much importance to them. It has been said that Danish courts often look at experts' statements just as the ancient Greeks used to look for answers from the oracle of Apollo. Often, as soon as an expert has stated his view the case is de facto over. It is certain that eventually the judge will conform his decision to the expert's opinion. It is not an exaggeration to say that the judge in fact 'delegates' some of his power to the expert witness.

Owing to the great significance that expert opinions have in Danish law it is extremely important to have a precise principle as to exactly how much can be left to the experts. It is urgent to define what questions experts can be asked and what questions must be answered by the judge alone, without the help of experts.

Such a principle can state only one thing: namely that experts are allowed to speak about the things they are experts on; it is then for the judge to deal with the legal implications. In short, the experts can deal with *technical, non-legal aspects* of a case, while the judge deals with the *legal aspects*.

In the child custody case the psychologist is the one to examine the psychological relationships of the family; the judge, on his part, studies the custody law before he decides which parent is legally entitled to have custody of the child. The judge is certainly not to offer anything in the realm of psychological analysis; that would be absurd. In the faulty machine case it is a matter for the engineer to inspect the machine with his measuring tools. Then the judge analyses the law and the legal precedents in order to find out how to decide in the case.

Expert witnesses deal only with their area of expertise: this is a basic legal principle in the Danish law of legal procedure. Therefore, experts witnesses are never to be asked legal questions.

See, e. g., *Hørlyck*, Syn og skøn, Copenhagen 1992 p. 11 where the author states that 'The legal evaluation can never be made by an expert; it belongs to the court. An expert only deals with the facts of the case', *Gomard/Kistrup*, Civilprocessen, 5th ed. Copenhagen 2000 p. 554 (states that questions to experts cannot 'concern the legal evaluation'), *Tjur/Høeg Madsen* in 'Proceduren', Copenhagen 1980 p. 162 f ('By the wording of the questions to the experts one must bear in mind only to ask technical questions as the [...] legal ones must be left to the court'), *Lindencrone/Werlauff*, Dansk retspleje, Copenhagen 2000 p. 245, *Gjesingfelt* in Proceduren p. 174 f, see also the decision of Sø- og Handelsretten in Ugeskrift for Retsvæsen ('UfR') 1986 p. 950, (stated that the parties were not allowed to obtain the opinion of certain organisations since the questions they wanted to ask were not concrete enough to make sure that the organisations only testified about 'actual matters rather than questions of law'), compare also UfR 1965 p. 216 H. The above-mentioned principle is being criticised by *Ryberg* in 'Julebog 1999', published by Copenhagen Business School, p. 187 ff. It is also assumed that experts who are being asked questions of law must refuse to answer or ask for a reformulation of the questions, and that expert opinions about such matters will not be used by the courts, see *Lindencrone/Werlauff*, l.c. p. 249 f and 252.

This principle, luckily, is also valid in copyright cases. The experts who are consulted in copyright cases are normally architects, designers, painters, carpenters, smiths, ironmongers, and the like.

See, e.g., UfR 1981 p. 946 H (two experts, of whom one was a carpenter and the other a furniture designer), UfR 1992.909 SH (one expert who was a designer) UfR 1972.992 H (three experts, one architect, one manufacturer and one who was both master smith and and engineer), UfR 1969.851 H (one architect and one ironmonger), UfR 1946.35 H (one sculptor, one plasterer), NIR 1965.103 SH (one painter, one master turner), UfR 1975.1014 Ø (one professor, one manager), UfR 1992.34 SH (one architect).

They cannot be expected to know about the intricacies of copyright law. Moreover, the aesthetic meaning of the words 'art' and 'originality', importantly, is distinct from their legal meaning in copyright law. A work which may not be 'art' from an aesthetic point of view can, in fact, be 'art' according to copyright law. Scandinavian courts have, for example, offered copyright protection to rubber trolls which were not 'art' according to the aesthetic experts (see UfR 1962.756 SH). By the same token, works which are probably 'art' from an artistic point of view are not necessarily art from a copyright perspective. Thus a Danish court once denied protection of a lamp despite the fact that the famous Danish architect *Børge Mogensen* emphasised its artistic originality (see UfR 1960.762 SH).

On the legal nature of the notion of 'work' in copyright law see *Schønning*, Ophavsretsloven med kommentarer, Copenhagen 2003 p. 92, *Wagle/Ødegaard,* Opphavsrett i en digital verden, Oslo 1997 p. 112, *Levin*, Immaterialrätten, Stockholm 1999 p. 64, *Schricker* et al., Urheberrecht, München 1999 p. 51 i.f., see also (regarding the legal nature of the notion of visual art) *Nordell,* Rätten till det visuella, Stockholm 1997 p. 65 f at footnote 7.

In a similar vein the concept of originality has a specifically, legal – that is non-aesthetic – meaning in copyright law. For example, it is often suggested in the copyright doctrine that there exists a so-called 'principle of unicity' according to which a work is original only if it is unlikely that it could have been created by two persons independently.

See for example *Schønning,* l.c. p. 107, *Olsson,* Upphovsrättslagstiftningen, Stockholm 1996 p. 33, 42, *Bergström,* Mélanges de droit comparé en l'honneur du doyen Åke Malmström, Stockholm 1972 p. 14 ff, *Levin,* Formskydd, Stockholm 1984 p. 296 ff, *Nordell,* NIR 1995 p. 630 ff and GRUR Int. 1997 p. 110 ff. The Nordic principle of unicity is to some extent inspired by a theory according to which originality is the same as so-called 'statische Einmaligkeit', formulated in *Kummer,* Das urheberrechtlich schützbare Werk, Bern 1968.

Furthermore, it is contended that the originality requirement should be 'strict' in connection to 'applied art', such as chairs, furniture and clothes, while the requirement is to be 'milder' with regards to 'pure art', i.e., paintings, musical works, etc.

See *Koktvedgaard,* Lærebog i immaterialret, Copenhagen 2002 p. 49 ff, *P.H. Schmidt,* Teknologi og immaterialret, Copenhagen 1989 p. 64, 69, 76.

The copyright principles concerning *infringement* – that is, the principles regarding the degree of similarity between two works that it takes for one to be a reproduction of the other – are purely legal, rather than aesthetic. For example, the so-called 'scope of protection' of a work is often thought to depend on the degree of originality of the work, so that works of modest originality have a more narrow scope of protection than works which have much originality. This again means that the extent of similarity which must be present before a work infringes upon an other work must be particularly large if the plaintiff's work is not very original, while it does not have to be so large if the plaintiff's work is a very original one.

See, for example, UfR 2001.747 H (concerning a baby chair, the protection of which was found to be restricted to 'very ... slavish copying'), *Schønning,* l.c. p. 118 f, Högsta domstolen, NJA 1964 s. 532 ff/NIR 1966 s. 74, BGH GRUR 1981 267, 269 – Dirlada, BGH GRUR 1988 812, 814 – Ein bißchen Frieden. From Anglo-American copyright law see, e.g., *Cornish/Llewelyn,* Intellectual Property, London 2003 p. 395 by footnote 83, p.428, *Gentieu* v. *John Muller & Co., Inc.,* 712 F.Supp. 740 (W.D.Mo. 1989) (concerning photos of babies, stated that 'In the case at bar, the plaintiff [...] has not expanded on the idea of a photograph of a naked baby [...] This is not meant to minimize the plaintiff's work in any way; its simplicity is its creativity. However, by utilizing her expression in such a way as to create a naked baby and nothing else the plaintiff limits her copyright protection to the identical copying of the copyrightable elements of her work'), *Kenrick & Co.* v. *Lawrence & Co.* (1890) 25 Q.B.D. 99 (drawing of a hand putting a cross on a voting card was not infringed upon by a drawing where the hand was a little different since very simple drawings were said only to be protected against exact literal reproduction, but that the plaintiff's drawing might be infringed upon by drawings 'in which every line, dot, measurement, and blank space shall be rendered exactly as in the original, or in which the variations from such minute agreement shall be microscopic'), *Apple Com-*

puter, Inc. v. *Microsoft Corp.*, 35 F.3d 1435 (9th Cir. 1994) ('When the range of protectable and unauthorized expression is narrow, the appropriate standard for illicit copying is virtual identity'). The above-mentioned principle is to a great extent based on the idea that in order to create a proper balance between the author and the society the former should not be allowed to monopolize simple aspects of his works, see, e.g., *Nordell,* Rätten till det visuella, Stockholm 1997 p. 60.

It takes extensive legal research to fully appreciate this matter, yet one is well-advised to keep in mind that, in the courtroom, the concepts of 'art', 'originality' and 'infringement' have legal implications that outweigh aesthetic judgement. A court, therefore, cannot decide a copyright case by leaving the whole case to the aesthetic experts. The barristers are free to ask for aesthetic advice from experts. In deciding whether something is 'original' in the copyright sense it is relevant to consider whether it is different from what is already on the market – and this is, to be sure, a type of aesthetic evaluation. Experts, however, are not to be asked whether, say, a given office furniture wheel is an original piece of art according to copyright law, and whether there has there been copyright infringement. This is essentially a legal question, which requires intimate knowledge of copyright law, including the special copyright meaning of the term 'originality', the specific scope of protection of works of applied art and much more.

How things are done in real life

In practice, the way Danish courts tend to deal with copyright disputes is to present expert witnesses with legal questions as well as aesthetic ones. That is, at some point the barrister asks an expert if the plaintiff's work is 'a protected, original work of art according to the Copyright Act no. 395 of the 14th of May 1995, article 1' or the like. Sometimes the infringement question is dealt with in the same manner, that is, the barrister asks the expert whether there has been 'a copyright infringement'.

See, for example, UfR 1960.483 Ø, question 1 ('Can arm chair no. 503, drawn by Hans Wegner and produced by the plaintiff, be considered an original work of art according to Act no. 149 of April 26th 1933 concerning copyright sec. 24), UfR 1972.992 H, question 4 and 5 ('Is the above mentioned fireplace a work which it has taken such an individual artistic effort to create that it can be called an independent and original work of art in the sense of sec. 1 in Act nr. 158 of May 31. 1961' and 'Is the fireplace marketed by Viking Varmeservice a new and independent work of art in relation to Niels Fagerholdt's fireplace?'), UfR 1969.851 H, question 6 and 7 ('Can the machine manufactured by the plaintiffs be considered applied art in the sense in which this notion is being used in the Copyright Act' and 'Has the plaintiff [...] infringed upon the protection given by the Copyright Act?'), NIR 1984.76 SH, question 1 ('Is the cross-stitch embroidery [...] made by the plaintiff [...] a work protected by copyright according to the Copyright Act?'), UfR 1975.1014 Ø ('Is [...]'Hurricane-lamp', – - – a work of art according to sec. 1 in Act no. 158 of May 31. 1961 concerning copyright?'), UfR 1992.34 SH, question 1 ('Can MONTANA be considered an original artistic work according to Act. no. 130 of April 15th 1975, sec. 1?'), see also for example UfR 1946.35 H p. 36, UfR 1963.782 H, question 1, UfR 1965.447 H, question 1, UfR 1968.189 Ø, question 1, UfR 1967.842 H, UfR 1968.785 H, question 1, UfR 1978.337 H, question 1.

Experts often end up providing answers to both the aesthetic and the legal sides of a case; the court bases its judgement entirely on the expert's statement. This is true, even in cases where the expert's answers demonstrate gross ignorance of copyright law.[1] However this is a clear violation of the basic principle that experts are only to answer technical questions: Danish courts, over and over again, deal with copyright infringement cases in a way which seems to be without principle. Firstly, barristers ought not to ask legal questions to architects and others who are not lawyers. Secondly, the courts ought not to accept this procedure. Thirdly, experts ought to refuse to answer legal questions if their expertise is not in the law. Fourthly, courts ought not to base their judgments on the experts' views if they happen answer to such questions. Nevertheless, many copyright cases have been decided in the way just described. I am familiar with only one case where somebody protested (UfR 1969.851 H). The case concerned a coffee mill which looked like an aeroplane, and the question was whether it had been infringed by another coffee

1. See for example M. Rosenmeier, *Værkslæren i ophavsretten* (Copenhagen: Jurist- og Økonomforbundets Forlag, 2001), p. 252-256, and M. Rosenmeier, Nogle bemærkninger om sagkyndiges medvirken i ophavsretssager, *Ugeskrift for Retsvæsen* 2001, part B, p. 102-109.

mill which also looked like an aeroplane. The lawyers asked two experts – an architect and an ironmonger – whether the plaintiff's coffee mill was 'a piece of applied art in the sense of the copyright law', and the ironmonger answered that this was 'a legal question which the court ought to answer'. Having said so, he answered the question anyway – as did the architect, without hesitation.

CONCLUSION

It is wrong – in fact illegal – to leave to laymen the outcome of legal disputes. Copyright cases often involve very large sums of money. For judges to throw intricate legal questions at architects, psychologists and engineers – who do not have expert knowledge of copyright law – and then base their decisions upon these statements is not a way of meeting a judge's responsibility.

There is no simple answer as to why court practice has deteriorated in this way in Danish copyright cases. Possibly it stems from the fact that many Danish lawyers suffer the misconception that the legal terms 'art' and 'originality' are readily translatable into their aesthetic namesakes.

To solve the crisis it is necessary for courts to address questions to expert witnesses in such a way that they are aesthetic rather than legal. In addition, Danish courts ought to reconsider the way experts are used in copyright cases. Barristers who conduct copyright cases ought to be more aware of the character of the questions that they ask. Finally, it is important that the experts themselves – architects, designers, engineers – who are consulted in copyright cases become more aware of the role they are to play. They ought to refuse to answer legal questions. According to the law of legal procedure an expert who is given a legal question has, in fact, a legal obligation to refuse to answer it. Such a joint effort is the responsibility of all members of a copyright infringement case; and it is the only way of returning credibility to Danish copyright law.

The Art of Giving and Taking:
A Figurative Approach to Copyright Law

*Marko Karo**

INTRODUCTION

The relationship between art and law can be approached from two viewpoints. On the one hand, art provides a fascinating means of analysing, critiquing, and commenting on law, justice, and other ethico-legal themes. In the absence of a more accurate notion, this could be referred to as *art's law*. On the other hand, the story unfolds to the other direction as well: it is evident that the law also has a considerable impact on art. It regulates, uses, and shapes art and the practices of the art world in multiple ways. This, perhaps the more usual (normative) course of events, can correspondingly be referred to as *law's art*.[1] In short, this dialogical and reciprocal relationship between art and law, between *art's law* and *law's art*, is the general concern of this essay.

In the following, I will trace the linkages between art and law by assessing the relationship between the law of copyright and photographic art (as well as other forms of visual art utilising the photographic medium). The focus on copyright law is here far from being a random choice. Indeed, and although mostly unacknowledged, in the diverse field of law it is somewhat exclusively copyright law that embodies an inherent and constitutive relationship with the production, reception, and appropriation

* *LL.M, MA*. The author is a Doctoral candidate at the University of Art and Design, Helsinki.

1. See, *e.g.*, Costas Douzinas and Lynda Nead (eds.), *Law and the Image: The Authority of Art and the Aesthetics of Law* (Chicago: The University of Chicago Press, 1999), p. 11, where a similar categorical distinction is drawn.

of art.[2] This is why it also needs to be addressed not merely as a rule-like structure conveying rights and obligations, but rather as a cultural political mechanism that has an acute role to play in the questions of cultural and structural diversity of the art world. Therefore, I will here approach copyright as a form of *art speech,* a juridico-aesthetic discourse that restructures the field of art and its actors. In so doing, my purpose in this essay is on the one hand to examine how the practices of contemporary visual art are conditioned by the politics of display of the law, and on the other to raise questions on the possibility of cultural and legal politics premised upon an ethical commitment to dialogic plurality and alterity. The central questions are therefore: what happens to a work of art when it enters the discursive space of the (court of) law? How can visual art guide the positive law?

As is evident from the foregoing, I will argue for awareness of both the aesthetic evaluative element in legal decision-making and the potentiality of visual art as a source of law. Naturally, this amounts to a certain departure from the conception where aesthetics, ethics, and jurisprudence are seen as distinct and autonomous spheres of discourse, as in both the Kantian tradition of philosophical aesthetics (which excluded both cognition and morality from its supposedly dis-interested and autonomous realm)[3] and in the legal positivism expressed in modernist juris-

2. While many fields of law (obscenity law, tax law, environmental law, public funding-related laws, etc.) have a bearing on art and aesthetics it is difficult to find other fields (outside copyright law) that would with an equal capacity partake both in the legitimation and delegitimation of artists (legal subjects) and artworks (legal objects) and in the regulation of the normative basis of the art market. The fairly common disregard of copyright matters in the Law/Art-related debates is reflected, for example, in the aforementioned book *Law and the Image: The Authority of Art and the Aesthetics of Law*: while legal architecture, obscenity law, and law's relationship with vision and images in general are all extensively addressed while copyright related concerns are categorically omitted, a fact that is justifiably critiqued by Anne Barron in her excellent review of the book in 'Spectacular Jurisprudence' (2000) 20 *Oxford Journal of Legal Studies*, pp. 301-315.
3. It must be noted here that there exists a plethora of irreconcilable interpretations of how Kant viewed the relations between the aesthetic, cognitive, and ethical realms. Hence, as Jay Bernstein has argued, even

prudence (which separated law from ethics and norm from judgment). Having said this, it is perhaps somewhat paradoxical to start the next chapter with a reading of Kant, namely, with his short essay on the philosophical basis of author's rights entitled *On the Wrongfulness of Unauthorised Publication of Books.*[4] However, as will be argued below, Kant's essay can be read as a basis for a tentative conception of law that is more open and sensitive to the demands of art.

Image / Property / Gift

Piracy and plagiarism were already acute topics of discussion in newspapers more than two centuries ago. The centrality of that debate is reflected in the fact that even Kant wanted to have his say on the issue, in the form of the aforementioned essay published in 1785 in the *Berlinische Monatsschrift.*[5] What is here particularly relevant in Kant's fascinating exposition is the clear-cut division he sketches between the respective abilities of literature and plastic arts, text and image, to merit copyright protection. Hence, Kant contends that whereas authors should have an inalienable and exclusive right to control the communication of their texts, pictorial artists, in their turn, ought not to be entitled to any exclusive rights to their works after their initial sale or communication to the public. From today's viewpoint, of course, such a categorical combination of textuality, pictoriality, and the

the very division between continental and analytic philosophy can (to a certain extent) be located along the lines of the respective interpretations of Kant's third critique, the *Critique of Judgment*: whereas analytic philosophy has received it largely as a defence of aesthetic autonomy, the continental tradition has read it more as 'the radical undoing of the categorical divisions between knowledge, morality, and aesthetics'. See Jay Bernstein, *The Fate of Art: Aesthetic Alienation from Kant to Derrida and Adorno* (London: Polity Press, 1993), p. 7.

4. Immanuel Kant, 'On the Wrongfulness of Unauthorised Publication of Books', in Mary J. Gregor (ed.) *Kant's Practical Philosophy* (Cambridge: Cambridge University Press, 1998), pp. 29-35. Hereinafter referred to as 'On the Wrongfulness'.
5. The article can be found reproduced from the original journal on-line: http://www.ub.uni-bielefeld.de/diglib/aufkl/berlmon/berlmon.htm

question of copyrightability seems somewhat surprising. Kant, however, had viable reasons for drawing this distinction.

According to Kant, a book is always characterised by a duality of two distinct realms. On the one hand, there is the material aspect, the physical corpus that can be freely used, disposed, and disseminated in various market transactions by the owner. On the other hand, there is an immaterial, intellectual element in a book that reflects the author's subjectivity, and which cannot be reduced to the logic of commerce. As Kant notes: 'The author's property in his thought [...] is left to him regardless of the unauthorized publication.'[6] For Kant, therefore, a literary work is divided between nonobjective subjectivity and a material medium that is opened to exchange. He formulates this incommensurable duality in precise terms: 'The author and someone who owns a copy can both, with equal right, say of the same book, 'it is my book', but in different senses. The former takes the book as writing or speech, the second merely as the mute instrument of delivering speech to him or the public, i.e., as a copy.'[7]

What appears to be particularly acute in the Kantian formulation of author's rights is *speech,* and its communication to the public. It is noteworthy that Kant views the authorial speech manifested in a book as an immaterial communicative act with an audience, fundamentally attributable to the persona of the author. As a result, in this discursive formulation authorial speech can never become objectified or alienated as a *thing* external to the self. One can trace the reason for this to the Kantian conception of the human subject: Kant posits a subject whose mental operations work spontaneously (rather than being causally determined) and who is also governed by a self-determining rational will. This transcendental, free, and autonomous subject surrounds itself with a material world comprised of cognizable objects ready for its intervention.[8] On this basis, for Kant, things

6. 'On the Wrongfulness', section 8:79, p. 29.
7. *Ibid.*, section 8:87, p. 35. For an excellent analysis of Kant's essay see, *e.g.*, David Saunders, *Authorship and Copyright* (London: Routledge, 1992), pp. 106-121.
8. See, e.g., Terry Eagleton, *The Ideology of the Aesthetic* (Oxford: Blackwell, 2001), pp. 70-101.

appear as objects *of* the will and therefore as necessarily different from and external to the subject. Speech, on the other hand, constitutes an *exercise* of the author's will and thus an internal and inalienable aspect of the authorial subject.[9] Significantly, the centrality of speech in this fundamental division between the noumenon and the phenomenon, the transcendental and the empirical aspect of a book, has several consequences for Kant's schematic formulation of author's rights.

First of all, Kant maintains that the right of the author is to be considered primarily as a communicative activity, not as a property right in a thing. In other words, instead of having the right to claim proprietorship of their self-expression, authors enjoy an inalienable, albeit clearly limited right of control of the communication of their discourse. Authors are vested solely with the right to authorise when and how their discourse will be communicated, so that their thoughts will reach the public in an approved form. It follows that, for Kant, authors have no right to control the *copying* of their works: only unauthorised publication of the author's writing is wrongful, not its unauthorised reproduction.[10] Second, the aforementioned Kantian schema implies that if the author's speech is no longer *as such* manifested in the work, its communication to the public can, correspondingly, no longer fall within the author's authority. Accordingly, Kant repeatedly emphasises that author's rights cannot be employed as restrictions of derivative works or translations. Thus, in Kant's view, one does not need the author's permission for publishing a

9. Anne Barron, 'Copyright Law and the Claims of Art', (2002) *Intellectual Property Quarterly*. No. 4, p. 399.
10. Kant further elaborates that the author can authorise a publisher to represent the value of the work, to publish and disseminate her/his writings: 'In a book, as a writing, the author speaks to his reader; and the one who has printed the book speaks, by his copy, not for himself, but simply and solely in the author's name. He presents the author as speaking publicly and only mediates delivery of his speech to the public.' (Section 8:81, p.30). The authorised publisher thus becomes an intermediary who '[carries] on an affair in the name of another', as Kant puts it. In contrast, the unauthorised publishers have no right to speak in the author's name: without authorisation they would force the author to speak 'against his will'. (Section 8:81, p. 31).

translation of her/his book, because the question is not of the *exact* speech of the author, 'even though the thoughts might be precisely the same', as he notes.[11] Finally, as mentioned above, it is against this background that Kant postulates the difference between the copyrightability of books and works of art, or, perhaps more appropriately here, between text and image.

Kant firmly stresses that the aforementioned duality between personal discourse and material form is not applicable to works of visual art. The reasoning for this is plain: unlike in literary works, in visual art the personal contribution of the artist is indistinguishable from the artwork's material carrier. Paintings, for example, are in Kant's view works that exist solely as tangible things, and, as such, they are only capable of attracting an ordinary property right in the material embodiment. Kant notes accordingly: 'works of art, as things, can be copied or cast from a copy that has been rightfully acquired, and the copies of it can be traded publicly without the consent of the artist who made the original [...]. For it is a work (*opus,* not *opera alterius*), which anyone who possesses it can alienate without ever having to mention the name of the originator [...].'[12]

What are we then to make of all this? What could be the relevance of the Kantian formulation of author's rights in the context of contemporary visual culture, where formalism and *l'art pour l'art* (to which Kant's name is most regularly attached) are nothing but fleeting notions reminiscent of the early days of artistic transgression? Certainly, the personalism underlying Kant's sketching of author's rights gives more than a nod towards what later became Modernism's fascination with autonomous and self-sufficient artistic originality.[13] However, as Anne Barron has suggested, on a more general level, Kant's account

11. *Ibid.*, section 8:87, p.35.
12. 'On the Wrongfulness', section 8:86, p. 34
13. For a juxtaposition of the Kanto-Fictian roots of author's rights with the Foucauldian criticism of singularity and originality see Gilbert Larochelle, 'From Kant to Foucault: What Remains of the Author in Postmodernism', in Lise Buranen and Alice M. Roy (eds.), *Perspectives on Plagiarism and Intellectual Property in a Postmodern World* (New York: SUNY Press, 1999), pp. 121-130.

offers us a radical alternative to the property orientation that characterises most copyright laws.[14] Indeed, the radical nature of Kant's arguments can hardly be overestimated in light of the increasing hegemony of the exchange principle (commodification) in the ongoing evolution of copyright legislations.[15] By dislocating the work of art from the realm of property rights and by emphasising the process-like communicative nature of author's rights (authors' moral rights) Kant arguably comes close to depicting a tentative frame of cultural politics that recognises the unceasing nature of cultural signification and articulation and rejects the fetish of equivalence which is of course inherent in property rights.

To revert somewhat, one can see affinities here with Theodor W. Adorno and Max Horkheimer's critical exposition of the relationship between the law (as justice), the image, and the exchange principle. In *Dialectic of Enlightenment* Adorno and Horkheimer accuse the modern notion of justice of blindfolding Justitia's eyes, of banishing images and placing the particular, the contingent, under the domination and commensurability of the exchange principle.[16] The question is thus of the disruptions, delegitimations, and (symbolic) violence on processes of cultural signification implied by a form of algorithmic justice, justice reduced to a law of equivalence based on the subsumption of particular cases under a general rule.[17] Significantly, even though

14. Anne Barron, 'Copyright Law and the Claims of Art', p. 400.
15. This can be seen for example in the unprecedented global-scale (WTO, WIPO, EU, USA) expansion of the economic rights inherent in copyright law during the past decade, as well as in the different political efforts to justify the expansion of copyright solely on the basis of the GDP-percentage of the copyright-related industries. See, *e.g.*, World Intellectual Property Organization, *Study on the Economic Importance of Industries and Activities Protected by Copyright and Related Rights in the MERCOSUR Countries and Chile* (Geneva: WIPO, 2001); Australian Copyright Council, *The Economic Contribution of Australia's Copyright Industries* (Allen Consulting Group, 2001).
16. Theodor W. Adorno and Max Horkheimer, *Dialectic of Enlightenment*, trans. John Cumming (London: Verso, 1979), p.17.
17. Martin Jay, 'Must Justice Be Blind?', in Costas Douzinas and Lynda Nead (eds.), *Law and the Image: The Authority of Art and the Aesthetics of Law*, p. 30. For a examination of the notion 'algorithmic justice' see

the image can itself fall under such universalising legal judgments, Adorno and Horkheimer emphasize its emancipatory, pre-lingual and pre-conceptual nature: the mute incommensurability of visuality, its mimesis, retains traces of a mode of (primal) interaction between humans and the world, subjects and objects, in which the former does not dominate the latter.[18] Unlike the text, therefore, the image can be, according to Adorno and Horkheimer, in some fundamental sense communal, resistant to the exclusivity and individuality of property. This is also something that the Kantian notion of author's rights seems to indicate: the idea that in a certain sense the features or properties of artworks are neither given by the artist nor belong to the work as such, but rather are reducible to the experiences of the spectator. It is arguable, then, that an ethically committed politics of (copyright) law should also acknowledge this phenomenological, process-like, and contingent nature of visual signification. What would such politics of law then look like?[19] Martin Jay provides us with the following suggestion: 'A different justice that would evade the binding force of the algorithm would follow the logic of the gratuitous gift, bestowed without an expectation of reciprocity […]. It would be incalculable, impossible to capture in definitions, irreducibly aporetic […]. This ima-

Alan Wolfe, 'Algorithmic Justice', in Drucilla Cornell, Michel Rosenfeld and David Gray Carlson (eds.), *Deconstruction and the Possibility of Justice*, (London: Routledge, 1992), pp. 361-386.

18. *Ibid.*, p. 29. See Theodor W. Adorno and Max Horkheimer, *Dialectic of Enlightenment*, pp. 17-42. *Mimesis* is a notoriously difficult and contextually dependent concept in Adorno's philosophy and thus too broad an issue to be fully examined here. Miriam Hansen notes the following: 'In the anthropological-philosophical context of *Dialectic of Enlightenment* the concept [...] involves a non-objectifying intercharge with the Other; and a fluid, pre-individual form of subjectivity. In this sense, the concept assumes a critical and corrective function vis-à-vis instrumental rationality [...]'. See Miriam Hansen, 'Mass Culture as Hieroglyphic Writing: Adorno, Derrida, Kracauer', in Nigel Gibson and Andrew Rubin, *Adorno: A Critical Reader* (Oxford: Blackwell, 2002), p. 64.
19. For an inspiring defence of an ethically committed politics of law see Costas Douzinas, Peter Goodrich and Yifat Hachamovitch, *Politics, Postmodernity, and Critical Legal Studies: The Legality of the Contingent* (London: Routledge, 1994).

gined justice is the basis not only of religious notions of divine justice but of every defence of a revolutionary 'political justice' that claims the right to suspend the prevailing laws of a system it deems unjust.'[20] Another, largely corresponding response would be to have recourse to the transgressive politico-legal potentiality inherent in the latter half of Adorno's well-known (Marxist) dichotomy between exchange value and use value, in which notions of play, plagiarism, and gift are also essential. Hence, as Ben Watson has noted: 'Any critique of exchange values (commodification) that has no place for use values (play) is doomed to failure.'[21] In what follows, I will concentrate on analysing the increasing topicality and need for a Kantian-inspired, minimalist approach to author's rights and for dialogical and transparent forms of justice in the context of contemporary visual culture. In other words, to ponder the relationship between copyright law, visual art, and the economy of gift.

Burning Bridges

When talking about the relationship between aesthetics, art, and copyright law one can without too much exaggeration argue that it is precisely the renunciation of the role and value of aesthetics and aesthetic judgments that forms the cornerstone of contemporary copyright laws, be it the continental *droit d'auteur* tradition or the Anglo-American system of *copyright.* Hence, the foundational concepts and principles underlying copyright law (such as the *author, work of authorship, originality, idea/expression* dichotomy, etc.) have been largely defined by the consistent efforts of the legislators and the courts to steer away from the subjectivity and inaccuracy inherent in aesthetic judgments. One of the clearest manifestations of this is the principle of *aesthetic neutrality,* aptly characterised by Oliver Wendell Holmes in the

20. Martin Jay, 'Must Justice Be Blind?', p. 31.
21. Ben Watson, *The Theory of Value in Marx and Adorno*, a presentation at 'Marxism and the Visual Arts Now: An International Conference', 8 April 2002, University College London.

classic case of 1903 before the US Supreme Court, *Bleistein v. Donaldson Lithographic:*

> It would be a dangerous undertaking for persons trained only to the law to constitute themselves as final judges of the worth of pictorial illustrations outside of the narrowest and most obvious limits. At the one end some works of genius would be sure to miss apprehension. Their very novelty would make them repulsive until the public had learned the new language in which their author spoke. It may be more than doubted for instance whether the etchings of Goya or the paintings of Manet would have been sure of protection when seen for the first time.[22]

Consequently, in order to avoid the problems of aesthetic censorship or having to embark on artistic interpretation, the legislators and the courts have spared no effort to limit their discourse about given artworks (or types of artworks) to their external manifestations, to the *description* of the artworks' formal and physical properties. The *idea/expression* dichotomy (common to all legal systems) entails that copyright laws primarily do not protect the ideas, thoughts, narrative, or motive in a given work, but solely the expression that reflects the author's personality. Similarly, the originality criteria as a precondition for copyright protection excludes aspects of artistic merit – works of both 'high' and 'low' art are assessed from an equal footing. On a first glance, then, and omitting the more than doubtful existence of any objective description[23], copyright appears as an aesthetically neutral means of promoting different forms of cultural expression. However, as said, this is only the initial impression. Any deeper assessment of the law's normative consequences reveals that it is at the root of the very emphasis on authorial singularity and value-neutral objectivity, the blindfold over *Justitia's* eyes, that the paradoxical relationship between copyright and visual art resides. In stark contrast to the premises underlying aesthetic neutrality, copyright law in effect functions much like an institution of 'art criticism',

22. *Bleinstein v. Donaldson Lithographic Co.,* 188 U.S. 239, 251 (1903)
23. Joseph Margolis has argued convincingly that we cannot aesthetically observe an object without simultaneously engaging in its active interpretation. See Joseph Margolis, *Interpretation: Radical but not Unruly: The New Puzzle of Art and History* (University of California Press, 1995).

placing different forms of visual art in unequal positions. First and foremost, copyright laws protect established art forms, such as painting, drawing, sculpture, photography, cinema, and architecture. At the same time, however, the requirements of authorial singularity and certain temporal and material stability often lead to discrimination of process-oriented art vis-à-vis object-specific artworks. Thus, copyright can implicitly exclude certain contemporary artistic practices, such as collective and performative art forms, body art and land art.[24] Similarly, the idea/expression dichotomy naturally limits the protection available to conceptual art and minimalism, where the work primarily corresponds with elements belonging to the public domain.[25] Last, but certainly not least, copyright law expressly delegitimates all those art forms that infringe its rules, such as politically committed appropriation art that *detours* pre-existing cultural signs.[26]

Against this setting, it is a truism to state that there is a definite gap between copyright law and certain practices of contemporary visual art. The law clearly legitimizes certain forms of art and delegitimizes others. And in so doing, it seems to be leaning towards an overtly modernistic notion of visual art. Significantly, therefore, the law is placed at the centre of a cultural-political symbolic struggle between owners and others, legitimate authors and their illegitimate alters. From this perspective, one can see certain affinities between the juridico-aesthetic discourse of copyright law and the discursive power effected by nineteenth century museums. Rosalind Kraus has elaborated on the latter:

24. See, e.g., Anne Barron, 'No Other Law? Author-ity, Property and Aboriginal Art', in Lionel Bently and Spyros Maniatis (eds.), *Intellectual Property and Ethics: Perspectives on Intellectual Property Vol. 4* (Sweet & Maxwell: London, 1998), pp. 39-87; Peter Jaszi, 'On the Author Effect: Contemporary Copyright and Collective Creativity', in Martha Woodmansee and Peter Jaszi (eds.), *The Construction of Authorship: Textual Appropriation in Law and Literature* (London: Duke University Press, 1994), pp. 29-56.
25. See, *e.g.*, Nadia Walravens, 'La Notion d'Originalité et Les oeuvres d'art contemporaines', *Revue Internationale du Droit d'Auteur* (RIDA) 181 (1991), pp. 96-165.
26. See, *e.g.*, Anthony Julius, 'Art Crimes', in Daniel McClean – Karsten Schubert (eds.) *Dear Images: Art, Copyright and Culture* (London: Ridinghouse/ICA, 2002), pp. 473-503.

> Aesthetic discourse as it developed in the nineteenth century organized itself increasingly around what could be called the space of exhibition. [T]he space of exhibition was constituted in part by the continuous surface of the wall – a wall increasingly structured solely for the display of art. The space of exhibition had other features besides the gallery wall. It was also the ground of criticism: on the one hand, the ground of a written response to the work's appearance in that special context; on the other, the implicit ground of choice (of either inclusion or exclusion), with everything excluded from the space of exhibition becoming marginalized with regard to its status as art. Given its function as the physical vehicle of exhibition, the gallery wall became the signifier of inclusion and, thus, can be seen as constituting in itself a representation of what could be called *exhibitionality*.[27]

In many respects, then, the court of law (dealing with copyright and art) acts as the modern space of exhibition: as the ground of a written response to the work's appearance in that context, and ultimately, as the ground of choice of either inclusion or exclusion. As a result, much critical writing has been devoted to the question of what causes the apparent rift between copyright and contemporary art. On the one hand, some commentaries focus on the author (the subject of law) and attribute this dissonance largely to the presumed hegemony of the Romantic notion of authorship in the copyright doctrine, which channels more protection to those art forms that comply with notions of artistic individuality, ingenuity, and indispensability.[28] On the other hand, other commentators seek to explain the rift by starting from the viewpoint of the categories of protectible works (the objects of law) and the particularities of the property institution, and arguing that there are acute similarities between the law's mode of defining artistic works and the way in which modernist art theory approaches art-works.[29] Certainly, and particularly when taken together, these explanations provide a compelling account of the reasons underlying the discordant relationship between copyright law and art. Thus, while it may not be well-grounded to insist on a

27. Rosalind Krauss, *The Originality of the Avant-Garde and Other Modernist Myths* (Cambridge: Mass., MIT Press, 1985), pp. 132-133.
28. See, *e.g.*, Peter Jaszi, 'Toward a Theory of Copyright: The Metamorphoses of 'Authorship', (1991) *Duke Law Journal* 455, and Rosemary Coombe, *The Cultural Life of Intellectual Properties: Authorship, Appropriation, and the Law* (London: Duke University Press, 1998), pp. 211-220.
29. Anne Barron, 'Copyright Law and the Claims of Art'*supra* note 9.

fundamental role of Romantic authorship in the structure of *Anglo-American* copyright laws, it is still evident that the individualistic ideology of creativity is alive and well both in the courts' discourse[30] and as a Barthesian mythical concept widely applied in various political strategies to justify the expansion of the rightholders' (usually corporations) economic rights.[31] Similarly, whereas it may not be fruitful to stress the similarities between modernist art criticism and continental law's mode of defining the protectible works, it is conceivable that the idea/expression dichotomy resonates with considerable modernistic (formalism, materialism) overtones in all copyright systems.[32] Yet, at the same time, these attempts to explain and rationalise the gap between law and art seem to be missing something: namely, the sheer clumsiness and rigid reactivity of law in the face of art's fluidity and transgressive potentiality. While, at best, art can be affirmative, engaging in questioning and rearticulating the normative structures of society, law appears, at worst, reductive and oppressive. As noted by Anthony Julius: 'Artists will always force the boundaries of what is held to be art; it follows that they will also

30. See, *e.g.*, *Rogers v. Koons* 960 F. 2d 301 (2d Cir. 1992).

31. For example IFPI (International Federation of the Phonographic Industry) effects political lobbying strategies where it invites individual artists (Jean-Michel Jarre, The Corrs, etc.) to explain on its behalf to political decision-makers, such as the European Parliament, how important the expansion of copyright really is in their view. (See http://www.ifpi.org/). Another clear example of how empty and meaningless the authorship-placate can be in the hands of major corporations is the WIPO Diplomatic Conference on the Protection of Audiovisual Performances (December 7-20, 2000): the collective effort to better the position of individual artists, namely actors, on an international level eventually fell down because of the unwillingness of the US to accept anything less than a regime including a full and automatic transfer of the actor's rights to the producer.

32. Anne Barron's analysis (quoted above note 9) of the deeper affinities between the definitions of the categories of protected works in the UK Copyright Act (1988) and Modernist, Greenbergian art-theory seems to hold true primarily *vis-á-vis* the UK system. Somewhat paradoxically, certain continental civil law systems of author's rights (such as the copyright acts of the Nordic countries) have opted for a much more minimalistic approach in which the categories of protectible works stated in the copyright acts are not defined further at all, but rather left to the courts' praxis (and even there the categories have seldom been discussed).

force the boundaries of what is lawful. Just as aesthetics lags behind art, so law lags behind aesthetics.'[33]

Perhaps, in light of the aforementioned, the conclusion to be drawn is that the acute aim should not, after all, be to speculate on the potential causes underlying the rift between copyright law and art, but rather to ask what should be done about it. Must the law continue to be tied to the never-ending role of the chaser, to the hopeless task of enclosing art? Certain commentators argue for an affirmative answer: that copyright law should continue its project of framing (reifying) the phenomenon of art by providing protection also to minimalism, conceptual art, ready-mades, etc.. Nadia Walravens writes: 'The law *must* thus extend its own frontiers to works that are recognised by all the actors of the art world: artists, philosophers, critics, writers, collectors, galleries, and institutions.'[34] Why? Why must the law remain in this age-old circle? And what kind of works are such that there could ever be a *sensus communis* in the art world as regards their originality? How would legal recognition and reification of the 'marginalised' and 'silenced' practises serve dialogic democracy, art's capacity to transgress and question? Indeed, to turn back briefly to the idea of (copyright) law as a space of exhibition, the arguments advocating the extension of law are to some extent comparable with those of visibility politics arguing for greater representation of the misrecognised, subaltern social groups within the gallery space. Both sides seem to believe that greater institutional visibility of the hitherto under-represented automatically leads to enhanced political power and economic status. However, in both political and cultural theory the viability of representation as adequate visibility

33. Anthony Julius, 'Art Crimes', p. 495, *supra* note 29. While Julius' somewhat exacerbating and romantic remark illuminates (and dramatises) the art/law divide it also reveals a seriously flawed conception of aesthetics. As a field of philosophy, aesthetics is not concerned with describing and analysing specific artworks, but rather examines more generally (and conceptually) the aesthetic experiences, judgments, and behaviour (based on both art and non-art) of people. Thus, philosophical aesthetics does not 'lag behind art'. Art history might do so, but not aesthetics. Similarly, law does not 'lag behind aesthetics', but is rather a specific context of aesthetic judging and experiencing.

34. Nadia Walravens, *supra* note 28, p. 128. Emphasis added.

has been repeatedly and convincingly called into question: moving away from the insistence on politics of representation towards processual and performative acts of participation both political and cultural theorists increasingly argue for unrealizable, unceasing forms of *radical democracy*.[35] Naturally, given the force and enforceability of law, the question retains at least as much importance in the sphere of copyright law as it does in museum discourse. Rosemary Coombe's remark brings the message across clearly: 'A truly dialogic democracy might be one in which we respect a prohibition on the commodification of some signifiers as commodities, to the extent that recognizing authorial possession of the signs of alterity may well suppress the ability of others to articulate social identity.'[36] In what follows, I will argue accordingly: a politics of law that is ethically committed to polyvocality and the possibility of an unlimited questioning in the visual arts necessitates not the extension of law, but precisely the opposite, narrowing both the scope and term of protection provided by copyright law. The photograph's entry into the courtroom, its passage from being an instrument of law (a piece of evidence, a piece of nature) to an object of law (copyright protected work, a piece of culture), provides an illuminating case for the pressing need to burn bridges between visual art and law.

Critical Exposures

Walter Benjamin begins his essay *A Short History of Photography* (1931)[37] with a description of the fog that in his view surrounds the early stages of photography. Benjamin contends that this fog,

35. See, *e.g.*, Ernesto Laclau, *Emancipation(s)* (London: Verso, 1994); Chantal Mouffe, *The Return of the Political* (London: Verso, 1993); Oliver Marchart, 'Enacting the Unrealized: Political Theory and the Role of 'Radical Democratic Activism', in Okwui Enwezor et al (eds.), *Dokumenta 11, Platform 1 Democracy Unrealized* (Kassel: Hatje Cantz, 2003), pp. 253-266.
36. Rosemary Coombe, *The Cultural Life of Intellectual Properties: Authorship, Appropriation, and the Law*, p. 297.
37. Walter Benjamin, 'Kleine Geschichte der Photographie', in Walter Benjamin, *Gesammelte Schriften II, 1* (Frankfurt am Main: Suhrkamp Verlag, 1977), pp. 368-385.

while not as thick as that covering the origins of typography, prevents us from writing a linear history of the photograph that would begin with the conventional phrase 'once upon a time'. Through this mist we can, however, perceive general points of departure which have a bearing on the dialogue between the photograph and the law. On the one hand, the early years of the photographic practice seem (to some extent at least) to be characterised by Renaissance-inspired notions of naturalism and perspectivalism aiming to produce objective images of the external world.[38] Louis Jacques Mandé Daguerre, one of the first photographers and the inventor of daguerreotype, emphasises this aspect of the photographic image: 'The Daguerreotype is not merely an instrument which serves to draw Nature; on the contrary it is a chemical and physical process which gives her the power to produce herself.'[39] In its infancy, then, photography was taken not only as a representation of nature, but also as its material part. On the other hand, it would be over-generalising of history to insist on the hegemony of the idea of objectivity even during the photograph's initial stages: it is conceivable that already from early on (1830s and 1840s) photography has been consciously utilised as an artistic media.[40] The result is of course well-known: the ontological core of photography is premised upon a dichotomy of culture/nature, or man/machine, subjective/objective, copy/original, untrue/true, if one will. Consequently, the ensuing debate on the photograph's artistic status with its notable opponents (Baudelaire, Lamartine, Bourdieu, Deleuze) and pro-

38. See, *e.g.*, Jonathan Crary, *Techniques of the Observer. On vision and modernity in the nineteenth century* (Cambridge: The MIT Press, 1990), pp. 133-136; Michel Frizot, *The New History of Photography* (Köln: Köneman, 1998), pp. 15-82.

39. Helmut and Alison Gernsheim, *L.J.M. Daguerre: The History of the Diorama and the Daguerrotype* (New York: Dower Publications, 1968), p. 81.

40. Early pioneers of artistic photography includes such notable names as: Hippolyte Bayard, Julia Margaret Cameron, Oscar Gustav Rejlander, Lewis Carroll, Henry Peach Robinson, etc. See, *e.g.*, Abigail Solomon-Godeau, *Photography at the Dock – Essays on Photographic History, Institutions, and Practices* (Minneapolis: Minnesota University Press, 1991). For an interesting thesis on photography's role in breaking the objectivism inherent in the Cartesian vision of camera obscura, see Jonathan Crary, *Techniques of the Observer: On vision and modernity in the nineteenth century* supra.

ponents (Benjamin, Kracauer, Barthes, Baudrillard) is one of the great narratives of the nineteenth and twentieth centuries. As expressed by one of the better-known opponents, Charles Baudelaire in 1859:

> It is nonetheless obvious that this industry, by invading the territories of art, has become art's most mortal enemy [...]. If photography is allowed to supplement art in some of its functions, it will soon have supplanted or corrupted it altogether, thanks to the stupidity of the multitude which is its natural ally [...]. Each day art further diminishes its self-respect by bowing down before external reality; each day the painter becomes more and more given to painting not what he dreams but what he sees. Nevertheless, *it is a happiness to dream,* and it used to be a glory to express what one dreamt.[41]

What is perhaps less well-known is that the courts of law have acted as central stages in this play of dichotomies. While it may not be fruitful to ponder whether photography is art or not, as Benjamin argued in his renowned essay *The Work of Art in the Age of Mechanical Reproduction,* it is a task the courts simply could not have avoided. From the mid-nineteenth century onwards, the photograph entered the (European) courtrooms not only as an evidentiary method but increasingly as a potential object of copyright protection. The courts were thus faced with a difficult ideological work of separating the instrumental use of photography from its function as art, drawing a distinction between man and the machine. It was therefore less in the internal quarrels of the art world than in the courts of law that the possibility of photographic art and the limits of its creative potential were determined.[42] In his path-breaking book *Le Droit saisi par la photographie* Bernard Edelman has analysed the perplexing and disquieting expansion of copyright protection of photography from the nineteenth to the late twentieth century. The initial claims for legal protection were denied by the (French) courts on the grounds that there was no requisite creativity involved: a photograph amounted to no more than a mechanical reproduc-

41. Charles Baudelaire, 'Photography', in Beaumont Newhall (ed.), *Photography: Essays and Images* (New York: MOMA, 1980), pp. 112-113.
42. John Tagg, *The Burden of Representation: essays on photographies and histories* (Basingstoke: Macmillan, 1988), p. 104.

tion of reality. As part of the public domain, it was conceived as common property. However, Edelman argues that as photography gradually grew into a considerable sector of capitalist production the viewpoints of the courts and the legislators started to change, not least because of the lobbying efforts of the cinema industry.[43] Eventually, then, in a 1959 case brought before the *Cour de cassation,* the court ruled that photography benefits from legal protection 'provided that it bears the intellectual mark of its author, the necessary imprint for the work to have the requisite characteristic of individuality in order to amount to a creation.'[44] Against this setting, Edelman contends that the courts subordinated the aesthetic to commerce. Juridically, the photographer was transformed into an artist, a creative agent, at the precise moment requested by the productive forces.[45] The courts utilised the notion of 'imprint of personality' to wrest the photograph from the machine and into the domain of the subject. In this light, Edelman maintains that photography 'freezes' the discourse of law. The law's functioning thus becomes visible in the expansive commodification of the real: as if in a still-image we can perceive how property is created, how creators are designated as artists and legal subjects, and how the domain of exchanges between owner subjects is designated as 'civil society'.[46]

Indeed, from the viewpoint of today, a setting in which the term of protection for photographic works is almost universally 70 years *post mortem auctoris,* Edelman's thesis is perhaps more acute than ever before. The 'over-appropriation of the real', the term Edelman uses to characterise the alarming diminishing of the public domain, is today a problem of serious cultural ramifi-

43. Bernard Edelman, *Le Droit saisi par la photographie: Éléments pour une théorie marxiste du droit* (Paris: Flammarion, 2001 [1973]), pp. 49-53.
44. *Ibid.*, p. 52. In clear contrast to France, the statutory protection for photographs came very early in the Anglo-American copyright system where creativity was not a precondition for protection (in 1865 in the US and in 1862in the UK). The Nordic countries as well as Germany also provided some protection to photographs in the nineteenth century. See, *e.g.*, Ysolde Gendreau, Axel Nordemann and Rainer Oesch (eds.), *Copyright and Photographs: An International Survey* (London: Kluwer Law, 1999).
45. Bernard Edelman, *Le Droit saisi par la photographie*, p. 54.
46. John Tagg, *The Burden of Representation,* pp. 107-108; *Ibid.*, p. 51.

cations. Paradoxically, while we are living in an age of an unprecedented flow of images, the possibilities for using them for politically and artistically transgressive purposes are increasingly limited. As aptly noted by Sven Lutticken: 'We have reached a strangely archaic state of civilization, where the ideal of emulation has given way to the taboos of copyright – as if Barbie and Harry Potter were images of gods guarded by a caste of priests, and to make unsanctified use of them were blasphemous.'[47] Naturally, and given the pervasiveness of the law's legitimating and delegitimating reach, the ensuing question is: what could be art's answer to this state of affairs? In what way could art's critical potentiality be channelled as a participatory critique of the law's monologic tendencies? This will be the theme in the following.

Lost and Found

Imaginary Homecoming is the title of a series of internationally exhibited works by the Finnish photographer Jorma Puranen. Puranen's photographs examine the history of the Sámi minority, their land, its ownership and use, and the changes in their social and environmental landscape. What is particularly important in assessing the images is the starting point of the series, a collection of archived photographs of the Sámi people that Puranen found in the *Musée de l'Homme,* Paris. As it turned out, the images were taken in the 1880s by a French photographer called G. Roche in the context of an anthropological expedition to Lapland organised by Prince Roland Bonaparte. Evidently, the original purpose of the photographs was to provide evidence for the supremacy of the white race.[48] To make a long story short, what Puranen decided was to photograph these historical documents and take them back to their original cultural setting. This was ultimately done by rephotographing the images, developing them on graphic film, mounting them on acrylic boards, and placing the

47. Sven Lutticken, 'The Art of Theft', *New Left Review* 13, Jan/Feb 2002, p. 90.
48. See Elisabeth Edwards, *Imaginary Homecoming: Photography of Jorma Puranen* (Helsinki: Kustannus Pohjoinen, 1999).

transparent boards in different compositions in the landscape and by photographing them again in their re-contextualised position.

Now, what concerns us here is the excellent, albeit regrettably rare example that Puranen offers of how contemporary art can constructively utilise pre-existing images as a political strategy. *Imaginary Homecoming* can be seen not only as a subtle criticism of political colonialism and Occidentalism, but also as a self-reflective critique of the colonialist and essentialist tendencies inherent in photography. Thus, the nineteenth century anthropological portraits exemplify a sense of representational colonization, a flawed understanding of the relationship between the real and the representational. Interestingly, it also seems to be this very aspect of visual misrecognition, denying of alterity and externality, which Jacques Lacan characterises as the 'belong to me aspect of representations, so reminiscent of property'.[49] Like the subject Lacan depicts as fortifying her- or himself against lack with the aid of a fantasmatic identity, the subject of copyright law, the author/rightholder, can also assume a proprietary relation to the world and freeze the play of signification by having recourse to her/his *exclusive* rights. Indeed, Puranen is bound to this normative setting as well. In effect, he becomes the 'owner' of the Sámi images incorporated in his 'own' photographs, the 'over-appropriator' of the real, in Edelman's terms. And this is definitely part of the captivating complexity of *Imaginary Homecoming*. The question is then: is Puranen any different from G. Roche, the photographer behind the Sámi portraits? Does Puranen manage to avoid the pitfalls of cultural essentialism? I would like to suggest an affirmative answer.

Borrowing a pair of concepts from Hal Foster, *traumatic illusionism / traumatic realism,* I would argue that Puranen is able to distance *Imaginary Homecoming* from the 'belong to me' type of possessive individualism that characterises much of contemporary cultural appropriations. On the one hand, in a gesture that echoes Benjamin's notion of the dialectical image, or what Fos-

49. Jacques Lacan, *The Four Fundamental Concepts of Psychoanalysis*, ed. Jacques-Alain Miller, trans. Alain Sheridan (New York: W.W. Norton & Company, 1978), p. 81.

ter terms traumatic illusionism (a critical piercing of the image-surface), Puranen places the screen of his 'own' photographs in a multiple dialogue with the documentary images as well as with the ephemeral image-surfaces that reflect through the acrylic boards onto water, snow, birch-bark, etc. The result, arguably, is a compelling and contingent constellation of temporal layers which extends our experiences of the present towards otherness, and in so doing converts the nature of dialectics from the synthetic to the non-synthetic. In other words, the lived experiences are not surrounded by closures, but instead remain open, and subjected to an unceasing play of re-evaluations. On the other hand, *Imaginary Homecoming* is also intensively underlined by a performative repetition. The evident shock caused by the first encounter with a camera appearing on the anthropological images is repeated in Puranen's technique based on rephotographing. As argued by Foster, the nature of the real as that which escapes representation necessitates politically critical art (that he terms traumatic realism) to revert to precisely this kind of repetition and copying (as in the case of Warhol's silkscreen images): the repetition both functions as the surface of the (traumatic) real and points towards it.[50] The continuous 'masking' of the Sámi people points towards the traumatic realism of photography's corporeal colonization. With these complementary strategies of criticism, dialectical juxtaposition and performative repetition, *Imaginary Homecoming* arguably stays true to its title and argues for polyvocal, fluid and unresolving politics of identities.

The particularly pressing issue here is that both of the aforementioned modes of aesthetic criticism are conventional targets of the prohibitive power of copyright law. It is no surprise, then, that Puranen works exclusively with materials that are in the public domain.[51] Why pay daunting sums in license fees, or take

50. Hal Foster, *The Return of the Real* (Massachusetts: MIT Press, 2001), pp. 130-136.

51. In a more recent series of photographs Puranen has continued his exploration of the picture surface by juxtaposing photographs with old paintings. He has photographed old (16th to early 20th century) portraits in a 'wrong' and anti-documentarist manner by purposefully letting the painted surface be covered with shadows, reflections, and gloss. As a re-

the risk of getting sued for illegitimate appropriation when one can utilise the public domain? The juridical results of such risk-taking are there. In *Rogers vs. Koons,*[52] a case cited in countless commentaries, the court (2nd Cir. US Court of Appeals) held Koons liable for copyright infringement after he had used Art Rogers' photograph without authorization as a model for his sculpture *A String of Puppies* to be shown in an exhibition entitled *The Banality Show.* Koons delivered a Duchamp-style defence arguing that his parody was fair use, because it was intended as a critique of originality, consumerism, and commodity fetishism. To simplify to the extreme, the court rejected Koons' defence primarily on the grounds that a parody can qualify as a fair use only insofar as the object of parody is the copied work, not a political or social situation. According to Judge Cardamone, this limit is required, because 'otherwise there would be no real limitation on the copier's use of another's copyrighted work to make a statement about some aspect of society at large.'[53] In other words, the art speech of the court here indicates the fundamental capacity of (at least US) copyright law to prohibit all those politically engaged forms of appropriation art that do not subordinate political critique to parodical amusement, and by extension, the status of the appropriation artist to that of the 'originating' artist, no matter how trivial and stereotyping the pre-existing material might be. Thus, artworks such as *Imaginary Homecoming* would have no chance of surviving under this reasoning. Indeed, Koons has hardly been alone in the defendant's seat: numerous politically active artists using pre-existing imagery (such as Andy Warhol, Elisabeth Peyton, Glen Brown, Barbara Kruger, Pierre Huyghe and Douglas Gordon) as well as the art institutions involved in showing their works have been subjected to the law's suppressing tendencies.

Whatever one may think of Koons' art, he managed, albeit unintentionally, to picture the workings of copyright law: how the

sult, the 'identity-fixing' conventions of portraiture are lost and the images opened to a more complex temporal co-existence between now and then.

52. *Rogers v. Koons* 960 F. 2d 301 (2d Cir. 1992).

53. *Ibid.*, at 310.

meaning of an artwork derives juridically solely from some mythic and exclusive point of origin, the bearer of the legitimate signature. In so doing, the Koons case also demonstrated both the curious silence prevailing in the art world as regards the law's negative ramifications and the entailing urgency for constructive and performative artistic efforts to question the increasing cultural homogenisation promoted by the law. Such efforts would be far from the egotism and commerciality of Koons and his appropriative contemporaries (Kruger, Prince, Levine), and would rather seek affinities with their radical predecessors of the 1960s, the Situationist International (henceforth the SI) or of N55 today.

Being a Marxist political 'movement' seeking a union between art and politics within everyday life, the Situationists had a somewhat complex approach to art. While the SI (initially at least) held the view that art and artists constituted an emancipatory social potential, it also set out to destroy the communicative conventions of the art world. In short, the SI aimed to replace consumable art objects with techniques enabling a simultaneous experience of the subjects and objects of art without any mediating factors. The central idea was the construction of situations, of 'momentary ambiances of life and their transformation into a superior passional quality.'[54] In the field of artistic experiments and art in general, the first five years of the SI were the most active as the best known members were primarily artists: Guy Debord, the French theorist and film maker, Asger Jorn, the Danish painter and CoBrA artist, Constant, the Dutch artist, and Michèle Bernstein, the French writer.[55] During this time the Situationists created a play-tactic termed *détournement,* a form of creative pillaging of pre-existing materials.[56] Taking their cue from Lautreamont's (Isidore Ducasse 1846-70) famous dictum

54. See, e.g., Guy Debord, *Report of the Construction of Situations and on the International Situationist Tendency's Conditions of Organisation and Action*, at (http://www.slip,net/^knabb/S/report.htm), p. 10.
55. See Stewart Home, *The Assault of Culture: Utopian Currents from Lettrisme to Class War* (Edinburgh: AK Press, 1991), pp. 31-40 (The SI in its heroic phase).
56. See, *e.g.*, Libero Andreotti, 'Play-tactics of the Internationale Situationniste', in OCTOBER 91, Winter 2000, pp. 37-58.

'plagiarism is necessary – progress implies it', the Situationists argued that critical art should be produced by applying the plethora of 'the literary and artistic heritage of humanity' for partisan propaganda purposes. The aim of the detoured paintings, films, sculptures, poem collages made by the SI was above all a devaluation and negation of the cultural past: fusing the most distant expressions overrides the original elements and brings about a more powerful synthetic organisation.[57] Hence, the evident distance to postmodernist appropriations:

> Plagiarism enriches human language. It is a collective undertaking far removed from the post-modern 'theories' of appropriation. Plagiarism implies a sense of history and leads to progressive social transformation. In contrast, the appropriations of the post-modern ideologists are individualistic and alienated. Plagiarism is for life, post-modernism is fixated on death.[58]

While the political aims of participatory activity in the visual arts today are naturally far from the drama and determinism underlying the Situationists' revolutionary agenda, it does not follow that the Situationist play-tactics and modes of criticism are irrelevant. On the contrary, it is arguable that precisely in the contemporary cultural setting with its preoccupations with visuality politics we need forms of artistic participation that are not so much political in their content as in their form and process. One interesting recent attempt of utilising (Situationist-influenced) communal, processual, and joyously playful modes of artistic critique in the context of copyright is a project entitled *No Ghost Just A Shell* by French artists and frequent collaborators Pierre Huyghe and Philipe Parreno.

In a manner resembling the starting point of Jorma Puranen's *Imaginary Homecoming, No Ghost Just A Shell* was initiated by Huyghe and Parreno in 1999 when they visited an agency (an

57. *For example a poem-collage on the Spanish Civil War added a fragment of a lipstick ad 'Pretty lips are red'. See Guy Debord and Gil Wolman,* A User's Guide to Détournement, *at (http:www.slip.net/^knabb/SI/detourn.htm); Asger Jorn,* Détournement as Negation and Prelude, *at (*http://WWW.slip.*net/^knabb/SI/3.detour.htm).*
58. Stewart Home, *Neoism, Plagiarism & Praxis* (Edinburgh: AK Press, 1995), p. 51.

archive of sorts) that develops animated figures for cartoons, comic strips, video games, *etc.*, to be used in the Japanese Manga industry. The artists became enamoured with one particular character, *Ann Lee,* a generic figure with no background and very few personality traits. Hence, given the Darwinism of the Manga industry where a figure's price relates to the complexity of its character and the ensuing ability to adapt to multiple story-lines, Ann Lee was a cheap figure destined to disappear very quickly. Like Puranen, Huyghe and Parreno then decided to save this discarded sign from the 'death penalty' of the archive shelf, albeit in a more collaborative way. Consequently, as a 'life-prolonging' gesture, the artists chose to purchase the copyright to the figure of *Ann Lee* (for $400) in order to give her a story, an identity, and a life of her own. To this end, Huyghe and Parreno released *Ann Lee* to the public domain, and invited other artists to contribute their ideas, stories, and contexts to the polyvocal and fluid mixture that is *Ann Lee's* identity. *No Ghost Just A Shell* is the culmination of these collaborative efforts by 18 artists in which *Ann Lee's* empty shell is filled with a plethora of significations in the form of video animations, paintings, posters, books, neon works, and sculptures.[59]

Naturally, one can argue that by purchasing the copyright for *Ann Lee* Huyghe and Parreno are in effect recuperating and participating in the copyright economy rather than negating it in a Situationist manner. Yet, in my view, such an argument would seriously undermine the transgressive nature of the gift in contemporary visual culture. From a certain perspective, one could see *No Ghost Just A Shell* as attempting a play of the exchange value/use value dichotomy with the aim of 'rescuing' *Ann Lee* from the sphere of the former. During the project *Ann Lee* would go through a fundamental transformation of identity from a commodity to a gift and in so doing partake in the formation of a community. Thus, whereas commodity exchange establishes quantitative relationships (equivalence of exchange value) between the objects transacted, gift exchange establishes personal

59. See, e.g. http://www.mmparis.com/noghost.html

qualitative relationships between the subjects transacting.[60] The collaborative efforts to keep *Ann Lee's* identity open and contested in the 'non-economic' sphere form a non-proprietary and contingent community premised upon 'the joy of public giving: the pleasure in generous expenditure in the arts', as Marcel Mauss puts it in his unsurpassed anthropological study *The Gift.*[61] The question is thus of a play, a certain kind of *potlatch,* a communal festival in which the community is affirmed by the consumption of the resources on which it relies, and in which the individual has to put forward whatever he/she has won in the play. Hence, the idea is not to provide for common property of the community (as in socialism or communism), but to keep the play of signification open: the gift must always be moving.[62]

One could also say that it is precisely the *figure* of *Ann Lee* that is the founder of the community. Drawing upon Benjamin's dialectical image the French sociologist Michel Maffesoli talks about the 'transfiguration of politics' based on our experiences of the image deprived of the representational task. In his view, we need a new means of analysis that enables us to think the real on the basis of the unreal. In other words, a means of rethinking otherness, community, politics, and the social via images and figures: 'The Figure is that which looks at us, which looks at me.'[63] Similarly, Jean-Luc Nancy argues that our incompetence in (conceptually) conceiving an open and indetermined community has placed Western political thought in a state of paralysis from which we can escape primarily with the help of art.[64] Echoing Nancy's thinking, David Carroll argues accordingly that it is precisely art that enables 'community to resist and exceed its own limits and ends, to be constantly undone by an alterity it

60. See, *e.g.*, Alain D. Schrift (ed.), *The Logic of The Gift: Toward an Ethic of Generosity (*London: Routledge, 1997), p. 2.
61. Marcel Mauss, *The Gift: The form and reason for exchange in archaic societies*, trans. W.D. Halls (London: Routledge, 1990), p. 69.
62. *Ibid*., pp. 5-7, 71-78.
63. Michel Maffesoli, *Maailman Mieli: Yhteisöllisen tyylin muodoista* (La Contemplation du Monde: Figures du style communautaire), trans. Mika Määttänen (Tampere: Gaudeamus, 1995), pp. 153-160.
64. See Jean-Luc Nancy, *The Inoperative Community*, trans. Peter Connor (Minneapolis: University of Minnesota Press, 1991).

cannot and should not attempt to contain or incorporate.'[65] Indeed, as noted earlier, this comes close to the theories of radical democracy. Against the notion of a clear and unchanging democracy advocated by Western liberalism, Ernesto Laclau and Chantal Mouffe argue that a democracy must remain unachievable if it is to be effective. Hence, in their view, democracy is an 'all-inclusive' horizon, an ever fleeing political signifier, which makes impossible any 'beyond'. As noted by Oliver Marchart:

> Which project succeeds in filling up the empty signifier or the horizon of democracy with its own content, its own demands, its own goals? The main struggle going on today, I would hold, is the struggle over the answer to this question. It is not a struggle between democracy and its other (that is, whatever lies beyond that horizon), but a struggle within that horizon and on the terrain of that horizon over the particular meaning and inflection of that very horizon. In other words: everybody is playing with the same signifier – the question is: which signified will be temporarily attached to it.[66]

In light of the aforementioned, it is evident that contemporary copyright law and the normative effects it entails are fundamentally opposed to the aims underlying notions of indetermined community and radical democracy. Indeed, perhaps *No Ghost Just a Shell* could then be approached as an imaginary homecoming to a setting in which the preconditions for the contingency and polyvocality implied by these notions would have been realised. It goes without saying that *No Ghost Just a Shell* is a project far removed from the radicalism of the Situationists. Huyghe, Parreno, and all the other artists involved work in the comfortable surroundings of the gallery and are not engaged in negating pre-existing cultural signs, but on the contrary providing new meanings and significations for them. Yet, one has to ask, whether this is a mode of criticism better suited for our times than the 'domesticated' *détournements* of the appropriation artists of the 1980s. Given the difficulties in foreseeing any systemic 'beyond', it is more than well-

65. David Carroll, 'Community after Devastation' in Mark Poster (ed.), *Politics, Theory, and Contemporary Culture*, (New York: Columbia University Press, 1993), p. 187.
66. Oliver Marchart, 'Enacting the Unrealized: Political Theory and the Role of "Radical Democratic Activism"', pp. 256-257.

grounded to opt for participatory and collaborative forms of critique from within the system, be it the gallery institution or the normative realm of copyright law. Thus, *No Ghost Just a Shell* provides us a welcome example of a local and collaborative attempt of *redefining* the horizon of democracy from within. Naturally, this does not mean that acts of appropriation would not be relevant in contemporary culture. On the contrary, it is conceivable that even the small-scale acts of resistance committed by millions of people on-line every day together constitute an overlooked and potentially emancipatory mode of participation which certainly raises questions about the legitimacy of copyright law on the Internet. Consequently, both modes of participatory critique are needed as countervailing measures against the law's hegemonic tendencies, acts of gift as well as acts of theft. It is to be hoped that the curious silence prevailing in the art world as regards copyright would be broken with more intense and public forms of copyright-related criticism, both inside and outside art institutions. Perhaps then, when there would be more examples of the acute relationship between normative openness and cultural diversity, there could be ground for a wider recognition of the cultural political need to move towards a more transparent, process-oriented, and non-proprietary normative setting – as elaborated by Immanuel Kant over 200 years ago.

Conclusions

Homesickness (Le Mal du Pays), the title of a famous painting by Réné Magritte, could well provide the underlying theme of this essay. What is it then that we can learn from Magritte in this context? Notwithstanding his known hostility towards any attempt to provide his paintings with explanations, the 'symbolism' of Magritte's works often extends a curious interpretative invitation to the viewers. Indeed, when looking at *Homesickness,* it is difficult not to embark on an exploration of its ethico-legal iconology. Tentatively, far from suggesting clear-cut interpretations, it is tempting to approach the work as a complex play between law, justice, ethics, and visual representation. As such, one could see it portraying law (as justice) as something inherently non-representable, non-achievable and groundless that we nevertheless long for, as something that is left in between the normative aspects of law (symbolised by the lion) and ethics (connoted by the image of the angel leaning against the railing of the *Palais de Justice* in Brussels).

Consequently, it is as if Magritte would tell us to stand before the law in the same way as we stand before an image: neither directly perceiving nor blindfolded, but always somewhere in between. Accordingly, as noted by Douzinas, Goodrich, and Hachamovitch: 'Ethics precedes law, it is the precondition and horizon of the political – of the making of law – while justice is the precondition of legality [...] the critical concern with the ethical is a return to the political and an embrace of responsibility: for the other, for the stranger, the outsider, the alien or underprivileged who needs the law, who needs, in the oldest sense of the term, to have a hearing, to be heard.'[67] Perhaps it is this 'being in-between' in which art can 'guide' the law. Here, as noted by Laclau and Mouffe, the ethical demand of art is precisely in the creation of an 'imaginary' of a system in which the conventional systemic problems are less likely to exist.[68] Hence, keeping the feeling of homesickness alive by creating a homecoming, an imaginary one.

67. Costas Douzinas, Peter Goodrich and Yifat Hachamovitch, *Politics, Postmodernity, and Critical Legal Studies: The Legality of the Contingent* (London: Routledge, 1994), p. 22.
68. See Ernesto Laclau and Chantal Mouffe, *Hegenomy and Socialist Strategy: Towards a Radical Democratic Politics* (London: Verso, 1985).

Some Current Issues Relating to Art and Copyright:

An English Law Perspective[1]

*Simon Stokes**

INTRODUCTION

Many artists are supportive of steps to increase the economic interest ('economic rights') copyright gives them in their works, whether by seeking royalties for the reproduction or distribution of their images etc through copyright collecting societies such as DACS (Design and Artists Copyright Society) in the UK, or through a share in the proceeds of the resale of their works, *droit de suite*. In addition to (and sometimes in substitution for) an economic return, artists also simply want acknowledgement – for their 'moral rights' to be respected – for example, to be credited when their work is displayed or published (the so-called right of paternity). They may also want to protect their work from 'derogatory treatment' – whether the publication of inferior reproductions, a dismantling of the work, its destruction, or the exhibition of their work in an unsuitable setting. So the artist wants strong 'rights' in a copyright sense; for the more innovative ar-

* Solicitor (England & Wales) and Partner, Tarlo Lyons, London; Visiting Research Fellow, School of Finance and Law, Bournemouth University

1. This paper draws on and expands some of the themes in the author's book *Art and Copyright* (Oxford: Hart Publishing, 2001; revised paperback edition 2003) ('Stokes') and includes items discussed in 'Categorizing Art in Copyright Law', 2001 Entertainment Law Review 179. The author may be contacted at simon.stokes@tarlo-lyons.com.

tist, there may be concerns that the protection the law gives lags behind what their creations need.

Yet at the same time artists also voice concerns that the strict application of copyright law potentially prevents the creation of works which parody, appropriate or are simply inspired by other works. Copyright law, rooted as it is in the concept of the single, identifiable author, is unable to accommodate works which reproduce substantial parts of others' works if the intention is to alter the context, parody or simply to create a new, distinct work. As a backlash, some artists have even gone as far as to follow the example of the open source software movement and have proposed a free art licence as a way to accommodate recognition of the author and to allow use of others' works free from fear of copyright infringement.

These two conflicting approaches are increased by the growth of the Internet and digitisation. Electronic copies can be effortlessly reproduced and published. Recent European laws intended to harmonise this area have strengthened the hand of the copyright owner, while moral rights remain outside of any attempt at harmonisation.

Various approaches may be made:

1. A 'self-contained' legal analysis looking at how current law protects art and the challenges the law faces[2]
2. An historical analysis of the development of artistic copyright[3]
3. An examination of the philosophical bases or rhetoric underpinning copyright and how these influence current developments. This might include the application of economic theory.[4] For example, copyright can be viewed in various ways including (a) in strictly utilitarian terms – as an incentive to

2. Professor Sterling speaks of the 'self-contained' approach in his *World Copyright Law* (London: Sweet & Maxwell, 1999).
3. There is much to be done in this area but see e.g. Bently and Sherman, *The Making of Modern Intellectual Property Law* (Cambridge: Cambridge University Press, 1999).
4. See for example William Landes, 'Copyright, borrowed images and appropriation art: an economic approach' in Ruth Towse (ed), *Copyright in the Cultural Industries* (Cheltenham: Edward Elgar, 2002) ('Landes').

authors to create and publishers, etc to invest, (b) as a right the law gives authors in recognition of their labours, (c) that works of art should be protected as they embody the author's personality or (d) a bold assertion that artistic works ought to be treated as property (in the copyright sense) and that copying is akin to theft.[5]
4. An exploration of current approaches to 'authorship' from a cultural studies perspective.[6]

As a paper written by a practising lawyer the discussion which follows is concerned with the first approach. Nevertheless even a pure 'legal' analysis inevitably sheds light on the underlying justifications that judges use for the enforcement of copyright and how the law defines 'authorship'.

The aim is to address some of the major current issues:
1. How the law categorises artistic works
2. Art, authorship and digitisation
3. Appropriation versus Infringement
3. Copyleft

The paper focuses on the economic rights of artists rather than their moral rights.

THE TREATMENT OF ART IN COPYRIGHT LAW

The Berne Convention expressly recognises that artistic works are to be given protection in member states of the Berne Copyright Union. Article 2 of the Berne Convention states that

5. Stokes at 9-23 discusses this.
6. See for example the work of Martha Woodmansee (e.g. *The Author, Art, and the Market* (New York: Columbia University Press, 1994) and Mark Rose, *Authors and Owners* (Cambridge, MA: Harvard University Press, 1993); to date, more attention to 'authorship' appears to have been given to literary works/copyright, than to artistic works/copyright. Maclean and Schubert (eds) *Dear Images* (London: Ridinghouse/ICA 2002) is a selection of essays from various perspectives on art and copyright.

> the expression 'literary and artistic works' shall include every production in the literary, scientific and artistic domain, whatever may be the mode or form of its expression, such as ... cinematographic works ...; works of drawing, painting, architecture, sculpture, engraving and lithography; photographic works ...; works of applied art ...

When granting copyright protection, most states do not discriminate between 'good' and 'bad' artistic works. So a work merely has to be an 'artistic work' rather than be above a particular threshold of quality.

In the UK artistic works are protected irrespective of their artistic quality: the Copyright Designs and Patents Act 1988 (CDPA) refers to such works being protected 'irrespective of artistic quality' (see below). The exception to this rule is works of 'artistic craftsmanship.'

The legislature and the judiciary have tended to shy away from making artistic copyright subject to a determination of the artistic merit of the work in question. For example in a recent UK case where engraved plates used to make rubber floor mats for cars were held to be 'engravings', the Judge was clear that UK law protects the majority of artistic works irrespective of artistic quality in order 'to deter the Court from attempting to answer difficult questions involving artistic judgment.'[7]

The classic exposition of the rationale for this approach is a frequently quoted observation of Oliver Wendell Holmes (as Justice of the US Supreme Court) in Bleistein v Donaldson Lithographing Co. (1903)[8] which affirmed copyright protection for a circus advertising poster depicting acrobats performing on bicycles:

> It would be a dangerous undertaking for persons trained only to the law to constitute themselves final judges of the worth of pictorial illustrations, outside of the narrowest and most obvious limits. At one extreme some works of genius would be sure to miss appreciation. Their very novelty would make them repulsive until the public had learned the new language in which their author spoke. It may be more than doubted, for instance,

7. Per Mr Recorder Christopher Floyd QC, Hi-Tech Autoparts v Towergate Two Ltd [2002] F.S.R. 15 (Patents County Court).
8. 188 US 239.

> whether the etchings of Goya or the paintings of Manet would have been sure of protection when seen for the first time.[9]

On this analysis even a modest work of art deserves protection because it will have the stamp of the artist's personality on it. To quote Oliver Wendell Holmes in Bleistein v Donaldson Lithographing Co. (1903)[10] again:

> Personality always contains something unique. It expresses its singularity even in handwriting, and a very modest grade of art has in it something irreducible, which is one man's alone. That something he may copyright.[11]

However as we will see below the courts do end up sometimes having to take views as to whether a work is 'artistic' or not. Otherwise the broad categories of work protected under UK law might be expanded too far to include functional, commercial items more properly the subject of industrial design protection.

UK Law

When considering the scope of copyright protection for 'fine art' the starting point is the Copyright, Designs and Patents Act 1988 (CDPA). To be protected by copyright a work must satisfy various qualifying factors regarding authorship or publication (not considered here)[12] and must also fall within a class of 'work' defined by the CDPA and be 'original'.

9. At 251.
10. At 239.
11. At 299-300.
12. For example as regards the place of first publication or domicile of the author. The author must in general have been dead for less than 70 years.

THE CLASSES OF ARTISTIC WORK PROTECTED BY COPYRIGHT

Copyright can only subsist in certain classes of works, exhaustively defined by section 1 of the CDPA[13] as:

(a) 'original'[14] literary works (includes any written work including a computer program)[15], dramatic and musical works;
(b) 'original' artistic works[16]: a graphic work (which includes (a) any painting, drawing, diagram, map, chart or plan, and (b) any engraving, etching, lithograph, woodcut or similar work)[17], photograph, sculpture or collage, in each case irrespective of artistic quality [emphasis added]; a work of artistic craftsmanship; a work of architecture (i.e. a building or a model for a building);
(c) sound recordings, films, broadcasts and cable programmes; and
(d) the typographical arrangement of published editions.[18]

13. It is an unresolved point as to whether only one 'copyright' can subsist in a given work – this issue arises from time to time primarily in engineering drawings and designs which often contain both diagrams and notation: for example in Anacon Corporation v Environmental Research Rechnology Ltd [1994] FSR 659, Jacob J held that a circuit diagram for a piece of electronics could be both an artistic work and a literary work (i.e. a list of components together with special notation for their interconnection) as under section 178 of the CDPA 'writing' includes any form of notation or code. This finding was criticised by Laddie J in Electronic Techniques (Anglia) Ltd v Critchley Components Ltd [1997] FSR at 412-413: either the information concerned is communicated graphically or by words. However the matter remains in debate: see also Aubrey Max Sandman v Panasonic U.K. Ltd & Matsushita Electric Industrial Co. Ltd [1998] FSR 651 and Mackie Designs Inc v Behringer [1999] RPC 717.
14. The issue of originality is considered below.
15. s 3 CDPA.
16. s 4 CDPA.
17. s 4(2) CDPA.
18. This rather narrow copyright serves to protect the 'image on the page' and protects the publisher (the owner of this right) who has incurred the costs of type-setting etc. from exact copying by photo-lithography or similar means: it protects the entire edition whether it contains a number of separate literary works or not (see The Newspaper Licensing Agency Ltd v Marks and Spencer PLC [2000] 4 All ER 239 at para 23 (per Peter Gibson LJ). [Designs for typefaces themselves are protected by artistic copyright – see below.]

Of relevance to this paper are 'artistic works'.[19] As noted above the UK Copyright Statute lumps various sorts of 'artistic works' together, some such as sculptures and paintings being more obviously 'artistic' in the sense of the fine arts,[20] others (such as diagrams, maps, charts or plans) being less so. This paper focuses only on works which fall within the CDPA's definition of artistic works. So video works or films are not considered in any detail.

As UK law is quite specific in the categories of artistic works that are protected by copyright, if a work does not fall into one of these categories it will not be protected by copyright. In fact, as one leading copyright Judge has put it, the law has been 'bedevilled' by attempts to extend the scope of these definitions.[21] According to another judge this is a feature of the lack of a developed law which protects against 'unfair competition' in the UK.[22]

GRAPHIC WORKS:
PAINTINGS, DRAWINGS, ENGRAVINGS, ETC.

The term 'graphic work' itself was new to the CDPA (s4(2)) but the definition includes paintings, drawings and engravings, defined in s3(1)(a) of the previous Copyright Act 1956 as artistic works. In Anacon Corporation Limited and Another v Environmental Research Technology Limited and Another,[23] Jacob J

19. No other attempt is made to answer the perennial question – what is 'art'? The UK courts define 'art' for the purposes of copyright protection in various ways, the category of 'artistic works' in the Copyright Designs and Patents Act 1988 ('CDPA') being crucial. For an early and very useful discussion of the legal protection of 'art' under English law see P.H. Karlen, 'What is Art? A Sketch for a Legal Definition' (1978) 94 LQR 383. Photographs, given their importance in modern art and their categorisation as 'artistic works' in the CDPA, are included in this paper.
20. *The Concise Oxford English Dictionary* (eighth edition, Oxford: Oxford University Press, 1990) defines the 'fine arts' as those 'appealing to the mind or to the sense of beauty...especially painting, sculpture and architecture.'
21. Per Laddie J in Metix v Maughan [1997] FSR 718.
22. Whitford J in Davis (J&S) (Holdings) Ltd v Wright Health Group Ltd [1988] RPC 410.
23. [1994] FSR 659.

said that the essential nature of a graphic work was that it was a thing to be looked at in some manner or other: 'It is to be looked at in itself' (at 662); here electronic circuit diagrams were held to be artistic works and also literary works. As discussed in this case, the visual significance of artistic works is important both in assessing their originality and also where a case of copyright infringement arises.[24]

Painting has its ordinary usage for the purposes of copyright and it is a question of fact in any particular case whether what is being considered is or is not a painting.[25] Drawing also has its ordinary usage and no particular artistic merit is required for graphic works: in Kenrick v Lawrence[26] it was held that there could be copyright in a simple drawing of a hand for a voting card but the scope of the copyright protection was very limited (to the exact reproduction of that drawing) as no one could monopolise the drawing of a hand in general. Another often cited case illustrating that quite simple artistic works will qualify for copyright protection is British Northrop Ltd v Texteam Blackburn Ltd[27] in which copyright was held to subsist in drawings for rivets, screws, bolts, etc.

It is worth speculating whether a random series of marks, say where an artist throws a pot of paint at a canvas, would qualify as a painting. If there was some order or selection behind the creation of the work (e.g. through the selection of paint, canvas, etc) there would appear no reason why not.[28] However there is old

24. See also Billhofer Maschinenfabrik GmbH v T.H. Dixon & Co Ltd [1990] FSR 105.
25. Merchandising Corporation v Harpbond (1983) FSR 32 (the facial make-up of the 80's pop star Adam Ant was not a 'painting' as a painting has to be on a surface of some kind: '[a] painting is not an idea: it is an object; and paint without a surface is not a painting' (at 46 per Lawton LJ). For a critique of this decision see Bently and Sherman, *Intellectual Property Law* (Oxford, 2001) at 63.
26. (1890) 25 QBD 93.
27. [1974] RPC 57.
28. 'Originality' ought not to be an issue as some skill and labour would be involved in selecting the materials and creating the work (see below).

authority to expect that if what is produced is 'meaningless' copyright protection may be refused.[29]

Rubber stereos for producing designs on transfer paper have been held to be 'engravings'[30], an engraving being held to include both the images made from the engraved plate and the engraved plate used to produce the engravings.[31] Likewise the engraved metal plates used to make rubber car mats with an anti-slip pattern, and the mats themselves, have been held to be engravings – an 'engraving' simply being an image from an engraved plate.[32] Certainly what is meant by the terms 'engravings, etchings, lithographs, and woodcuts' depends upon how the processes (engraving, etching, etc) are defined.

For example, could a mould or a die as such be an 'engraving'? This was doubted by the Hong Kong Court of Appeal per Fuad JA in Interlego AG v Tyco Industries Inc.[33] commenting on a New Zealand case where 'engraving' included the mould to make a 'Frisbee'.[34] In the 'Frisbee' case the injection moulds were considered to be engravings as the moulds had been cut to produce the ribs or rings on a Frisbee. However not all cutting of metal is engraving: cutting a metal rod into sections would not be engraving; engraving in the words of one judge 'has to do with marking, cutting or working the surface—typically a flat

29. Fournet v Pearson Ltd (1897) 14 T.L.R. 82, (CA) (unintelligible drunken scrawl). However the authority of this case must be doubted – it concerned an alleged literary work written by drunk optician and published after the event 'for scientific purposes': the test for a literary work was held by the Judge at trial to be whether 'it was something of enduring benefit to mankind.' The Court of Appeal gave no consideration to the question of subsistence of copyright.
30. James Arnold and Co. Limited v Miafern and Others [1980] RPC 397.
31. At 403. Paul Baker Q.C. was also of the view that an engraving need not just be made by an engraving process (i.e. cutting into wood, metal or other material) (at 403).
32. Hi-Tech Autoparts Ltd v Towergate Two Ltd (No. 2) [2002] F.S.R. 16, following James Arnold and Co Limited v Miafern and the 'Frisbee' case (Wham-O Manufacturing Co v Lincoln Industries Ltd [1985] R.P.C. 127).
33. [1987] FSR 409 at 453.
34. Wham-O Manufacturing Co. v Lincoln Industries Ltd [1985] RPC 127 (CA).

surface—of an object.'[35](35) In any event where a mould is used a sculpture might be the result.

PHOTOGRAPHS

'Photograph' is defined under the CDPA (s4(2)) as 'a recording of light or other radiation on any medium on which an image is produced or from which an image may by any means be produced, and which is not part of a film'. Photography is a problem for copyright law. In a sense every photograph is a copy of something. Unlike drawing or painting the actual recording of the image can require no skill or labour beyond the mere mechanical operation of a 'point and shoot' camera: it is asked, can photographs be 'original' in order to qualify for copyright protection?

Certainly UK law is more generous in its protection of photographs than the authors' rights or *droit d'auteur* systems. The courts recognised photography as 'fine art' early on.[36] In UK law there is much scope for 'originality' in a photograph: for example, the use of specialised techniques such as angle of shot, exposure and use of filters; the creation of a specific scene or style of subject; and merely being in the right place at the right time. These factors all contribute to the creation of an original work. As discussed below, only a low level of originality is required in UK law; that some, albeit limited work or effort has gone into the creation of the work is enough. A photograph of an engraving from a picture, for example, has been held to be an 'original' photograph worthy of copyright protection.[37]

35. Per Pincus J in Greenfield Products Pty Ltd v Rover-Scott Bonnar Ltd (1990) 17 I.P.R. 417 (Federal Court of Australia), approved in Hi-Tech Autoparts Ltd v Towergate Two Ltd [2002] F.S.R. 15 at para 41.
36. 'It is to be remarked that this Act of Parliament [Fine Art Copyright Act 1862] treats photography as a fine art' (per Bowen LJ) in Nottage v Jackson L.R.11 Q.B. Div 627 (1883).
37. Graves' Case (1869) LR 4 QB 715 is the authority for this. See Stokes n.1 above for a discussion of this case in light of two recent cases involving the subsistence of copyright in photographs of 'public domain' paintings and antiques: The Bridgeman Art Library Ltd v Corel Corporation (February 26, 1999, US District Court, SOUTHERN DISTRICT

Sculptures/Ready-mades/Collages

'Sculpture' is not defined by the CDPA, except that it includes 'any cast or model made for the purposes of sculpture.'[38] So sculpture for the purposes of the CDPA is a sculpture in the ordinary sense of the term or any cast or model made for the purposes of sculpture. It appears possible that objects other than what one would traditionally class as 'sculpture' may nevertheless be sculptures for the purpose of copyright protection; in the New Zealand 'Frisbee' case noted above a carved wooden model of the 'Frisbee' was held to be a sculpture. However the manufactured plastic flying discs themselves were considered utilitarian objects lacking 'any expressive form of the creator and any idea which the creator seeks to convey' – according to the judge, 'sculpture should in three-dimensional form express the idea of the sculptor.'[39] In a later case models and casts for dental impression trays were held not to be sculptures as they were not made for the purposes of sculpture, were merely steps in the production process and it was never intended that they have any continuing existence.[40]

In any event the extension of 'sculpture' to include what are properly industrial designs (e.g. in Breville Europe Ltd v Thorn EMI Domestic Appliances Ltd[41] plaster shapes made to produce

OF NEW YORK; Lewis A. Kaplan J, 97 Cir.6232 (LAK) (The case is reported in *New York Law Journal* 24 February, 1999) and Antiquesportfolio.com plc v Rodney Fitch and Co Ltd, The Times 21 July, 2000 (Chancery Division; Neuberger J).

38. S.4(2) CDPA.
39. Wham-O Manufacturing Co. v Lincoln Industries Ltd. [1985] RPC 127, at 157 (per Davison CJ).
40. J&S Davis (Holdings) Limited v Wright Health Group Limited [1988] RPC 403.
41. [1995] FSR 77 (a case in fact decided by Falconer J in 1985). The manner in which the work was made was held to be important e.g. carving, modelling or casting are all part of the process of making a sculpture based on the ordinary dictionary meaning of sculpture (from the Concise Oxford Dictionary) as extended by s48(1) of the 1956 Act (which extended sculpture to include 'any cast or model made for the purposes of sculpture') (at 94); this approach was followed by Lloyd J in Creation Records v News Group Newspapers, The Times 29 April 1997; [1997] EMLR 445, who stated that the assembly of objets trouvés in that case could not be a sculpture on this basis.

die-casting moulds for the heating plates of a sandwich toaster were held to be sculptures) may be receding (or at least it was until Hi-Tech Autoparts (see below)).

Later case law (Metix (UK) Limited and Another v G.H. Maughen (Plastics) Limited and Another[42]) has suggested that the courts will tend to interpret 'sculpture' in its ordinary sense – 'a three dimensional work made by an artist's hand.'[43] This case concerned inter alia moulds for making cartridges (used to mix chemicals) which the plaintiffs claimed copyright in as works of sculpture. This was firmly rejected by the Judge, Laddie J, on the basis that although it was not possible to say with precision what is and what is not a sculpture, the persons making the moulds did not appear to consider themselves (nor were they considered by anyone else) to be artists when they designed the moulds, and their only considerations in making the moulds was to achieve a precise functional effect rather than any aesthetic appeal. To describe the moulds as sculptures would be to go far beyond the meaning which the word 'sculpture' has for ordinary members of the public, notwithstanding the frequent attempts made to widen the field covered by the Copyright Acts.

However the approach of Laddie J in Metix was criticised in a recent case, Hi-Tech Autoparts Limited v Towergate Two Ltd[44], where it was held that any attempt by a Court to answer difficult questions of artistic judgment had to be avoided, certainly in the case of graphic works including engravings (where the definition of graphic works included such utilitarian works as diagrams, charts and plans) and also in the case of sculptures which were to be protected 'irrespective of artistic quality.'[45]

Hi-Tech Autoparts eschews any attempt to assess whether a work is 'artistic' in the broadest sense, this leads to the absurd result that a mass produced rubber car mat is an engraving. An earlier Australian case declined to hold that the drive mechanism of a lawnmower was an engraving: 'no consideration of policy, or other orthodox approach, could justify straining the

42. [1997] FSR 718.
43. Per Laddie J.
44.[2002] F.S.R. 15.
45. At para 47.

English language so far as to call the moulds [of a lawnmower engine] engravings.'[46] Prior to Hi-Tech Autoparts the courts in the view of two leading commentators were becoming 'more willing to use a general sense of what is meant by art to limit the scope of protectable works.'[47]

Looking more specifically at art rather than industrial design, in Creation Records Ltd. and others v. News Group Newspapers Ltd[48], it was argued that the scene of assembled objects in a swimming pool together with the members of the Oasis pop group which was to form the subject matter of an album cover photograph was itself an artistic work, either a sculpture, collage or work of artistic craftsmanship. The judge gave short shrift to it being a sculpture or a work of artistic craftsmanship as, citing Breville, no element in the composition had been carved, modelled or made in any of the other ways in which sculpture is made. Nor did it appear to involve the exercise of any craftsmanship.[49]

However the judge in Creation Records did discuss at greater length the possible meaning of 'collage' under the CDPA. 'Collage' was introduced into the CDPA in 1988 as a new category of artistic work. According to Lloyd J, the traditional understanding of that word is that it involves the use of glue or some other adhesive in the process of making a work of visual art, being derived from the French, although the Concise Oxford Dictionary 9th edition also defined it as 'a collection of unrelated things.' Lloyd J was firmly of the view that an essential element of a collage is the sticking of two or more things together; the collocation of random, unfixed elements (as in the photograph) was not a collage even if done with artistic intent.[50]

The judge's discussion of whether the composition in question was a 'collage' is worth reading. Counsel for the Plaintiffs had argued that s4 of the CDPA ought not to be construed to

46. Greenfield Products Pty Ltd v Rover-Scott Bonnar Ltd (1990) 17 IPR 417 (Fed Ct).
47. Bently and Sherman, *Intellectual Property Law* (Oxford, 2001) at 63.
48. *The Times* 29 April 1997; [1997] EMLR 445.
49. At 448-449.
50. At 450.

deny copyright protection to novel works of art. So Lloyd J considered, in passing, the possible copyright treatment of a number of contemporary art works difficult to categorise within the existing definitions of works protected by copyright. These included Carl Andre's bricks, the stone circles created by Richard Long, Rachel Whiteread's house, the living sculptures of Gilbert and George and installation art generally. In the end he did not find it necessary or appropriate to determine the matter. However he did distinguish the record cover 'compilation' or assembled scene from such works of art on the basis that the 'compilation' was merely, indeed intrinsically, ephemeral, and was materially different from such works of art.[51]

A WORK OF ARTISTIC CRAFTSMANSHIP

The courts have had difficulty defining this category of work which expressly includes 'artistic' in its definition. Its introduction into English copyright law in the 1911 Copyright Act[52] appears to have been a response to the Arts and Crafts Movement. It would cover the work of an artist-craftsman and include such items as hand-painted tiles, stained-glass windows, wrought-iron gates and certain pieces of furniture.[53] As nine separate approaches to the definition of 'work of artistic craftsmanship' are

51. At 449-450. Nor was it a 'dramatic work' as it was inherently static, having no movement, story or action (at 448). The judge in fact rejected all attempts to claim that the 'composition' assembled for the photograph was a work protected by copyright. However he did consider that there was an arguable case that the taking of the photograph and its publication was in breach of confidence (the composition had been made at a hotel under conditions of security and limited access).
52. S35.
53. See George Hensher Ltd v Restawile Upholstery (Lancs) Ltd (1975) RPC 31, the leading case, in which the House of Lords considered the availability of copyright protection for the prototype model of a drawing room furniture suite comprising two chairs and a settee. The House of Lords unanimously determined that the prototype furniture did not fall within the definition of a 'work of artistic craftsmanship' within s3(1)(c) of the Copyright Act 1956. This case has been the subject of much comment: see for example David Booton, 'Art in the Law of Copyright: Legal Determinations of Artistic Merit under United Kingdom Copyright Law', [1996] 1 ARTL 125.

discernible from the leading case, Hensher,[54] the law is, to say the least, uncertain. For example, Lords Simon and Kilbrandon considered that the intention of the maker to create a work of art was highly significant.[55] Lord Reid, however, whilst regarding the intention of the designer as important, did not consider this conclusive, nor was the utility of the work a bar to protection. The work must clearly be made by craftsmanship[56] and in determining whether it is 'artistic' it is important to avoid philosophical concerns of aesthetics, not least because those ignorant about philosophy are entitled to have opinions about what is artistic.[57] Lord Reid was also of the view that a work was 'artistic' if a substantial section of the public genuinely admires and values it for its appearance and gets pleasure or satisfaction, whether emotional or intellectual, from looking at it, whether or

54. See above.
55. In Hensher, Lord Simon was also of the view that 'works of artistic craftsmanship' must be construed as a whole (and artistic and craftsman not construed in isolation (at 69)) and furthermore it could not be properly construed without bearing in mind the aims and achievements of the Arts and Crafts Movement with its emphasis on the applied or decorative (as opposed to the fine) arts, although craftsmanship is not limited to handicraft nor is 'artistic' incompatible with machine production (at 66). It did however presuppose special training, skill and knowledge for its production (at 66 – Lord Simon cited Cuisenaire v Reed [1963] VR 719 and Cuisenaire v S.W. Imports Ltd [1968] 1 Ex CR 493 at 514). Ultimately what was important was, is the work by someone who in this respect was an artist-craftsman? (at 69), and given the presence of craftsmanship, what was the intent of the creator and the result of their work? (at 70) ('artists have vocationally an aim and impact which differ from those of the ordinary run of humankind' (at 70)). See also the later Australian case of Komesaroff v Mickle and Others [1988] RPC 204 (a product for creating moving sand pictures was held not to be a work of artistic craftsmanship as no craftsmanship on the part of the creator was employed in creating the product (Cuisenaire v Reed was also applied although Hensher was not cited)). Lord Kilbrandon was also of the view that the conscious intention of the craftsman was the primary test of whether his product is artistic or not: 'the fact that many of us like looking at a piece of honest work, especially in the traditional trades, is not enough to make it a work of art' (at 71).
56. At 53 – Lord Reid was of the view this suggests a durable handmade object and not something, for example, to be used merely as a step in a commercial operation which has no value in itself.
57. At 54.

not others consider it vulgar or common or meaningless.[58] Lord Morris said that to decide whether a work fell within the definition, the work must itself be assessed in a detached and objective way to determine whether it has the character or virtue of being artistic, without giving decisive weight to the author's intention (although this was a possible pointer). It was a question of fact upon which the court should pay heed to the evidence adduced.[59] Viscount Dilhorne was also of the view that the functional appeal of a work was not a bar to protection: for him it was simply a question of fact for the judge and 'works of artistic craftsmanship' must be given its ordinary and natural meaning.[60]

Subsequent cases to Hensher do little to clarify things. In Merlet v Mothercare plc[61] Walton J denied protection to a baby rain-cosy as the creator, Mme Merlet had designed it without any artistic consideration in mind but rather to protect her baby on a visit to Scotland from 'the assumed rigours of a Highland summer'[62]; also, following Lord Reid and others in Hensher, the onlooker gained no aesthetic satisfaction from contemplating the garment, which was also relevant.[63] In Shelley Films Limited v Rex Features Limited[64] Merlet was distinguished and it was held to be arguable that copyright could subsist in a film set as a work of artistic craftsmanship.[65] Creation Records Limited and

58. At 54.
59. At 57.
60. At 62. Like Lord Reid he was also of the view that a work of craftsmanship is something made by hand and not mass produced (at 60). Note however that in light of the development of the Arts and Crafts Movement as noted above Lord Simon was of the view that 'craftsmanship' was not limited to handicraft (but it did presuppose special training, skill and knowledge for its production) nor was 'artistic' incompatible with machine production (at 66).
61. [1986] RPC 115.
62. At 126-127.
63. At 124. It was not permissible to consider the article in its intended use (i.e. mother, baby and raincosy together as an ensemble); to determine the question the article must be judged on its own merits (at 124).
64. [1994] EMLR 134 (application for interlocutory relief).
65. If the set were imaginatively conceived and implemented overall and the overall effect and intent was artistic (at 143).

Others v News Group Newspapers Limited[66] also considered Shelley Films: the assembly of 'objets trouvés' photographed in Creation Records was held not to be a work of 'artistic craftsmanship' – it was not the subject of or result of the exercise of any craftsmanship,[67] and it could be distinguished from a film set (as in Shelley Films) which clearly does involve craftsmanship in its creation.

However in the New Zealand case Bonz Group (Pty) Ltd v Cooke,[68] Tipping J had to consider whether hand-knitted woollen sweaters and cardigans designed and knitted by different persons depicting among other things dancing lambs and golfing kiwis were entitled to protection as works of artistic craftsmanship: the Judge held they were.[69] Bonz was recently applied in the UK in Vermaat v Boncrest Ltd[70] which concerned sample patchwork bedspreads which were held not to be works of artistic craftsmanship: following Bonz it was necessary to consider whether they could fairly be said to be the work of both a crafts-

66. [1997] E.M.L.R. 444 (another application for an interlocutory injunction).
67. See especially Lord Simon in Hensher.
68. [1994] 3 NZLR 216.
69. Consideration was given to Hensher, Merlet, Cuisenaire v Reed and the earlier dress design case of Burke and Margot Burke Limited v Spicers Dress Designs [1936] Ch 400 (which denied protection to a woman's dress on the basis it was a work of artistic craftsmanship (skilled dressmakers derived their ideas from a design sketch made by a director of the plaintiff – a case doubted by Oliver J in Radley Gowns Ltd v Costas Spyrou [1975] FSR 455 where it was found to be arguable that the original dress was a work of artistic craftsmanship)). Tipping J had difficulty with making the intention of the designer the determinative test – there had to be an objective element – there must be some artistic quality present. What was important was that the author was both a craftsman and an artist: a craftsman makes something in a skilful way and takes justified pride in their workmanship; an artist has creative ability who produces something with creative appeal. The idea of craftsmanship relates more to the execution of the work than its design but 'artistic' relates more to the design and it did not matter that the designer and craftsman were different persons (at 224).
70. The Times, 23 June, 2000 (Ch D, Evans-Lombe J); [2000] EIPR N-151; [2001] FSR 5; Intellectual Property Lawyer Issue 3, July 2000. Hensher was considered by Evans-Lombe J but the approach of Tipping J in Bonz was the one he actually applied.

man and an artist; in this case the bedspreads could not be viewed as artistic or creative enough to fall within the definition of a work of artistic craftsmanship.[71] The court did not consider the talents and intentions of the designer.[72]

In another recent case (Shirin Guild v Eskandar Limited)[73] the judge (Rimer J) followed Merlet v Mothercare in determining whether the plaintiff's garments were works of artistic craftsmanship: Rimer J expressed the test as twofold. First, that their creation manifested an exercise of craftsmanship; second, that they are works of art (a matter of evidence: a primary consideration here but not necessarily the only one being whether or not their maker had the conscious purpose of creating a work of art and if he did it will be a work of art).[74]

In contrast with all these cases is an Australian case Coogi Australia v Hysport International (1999) 157 ALR 247 (Federal Court of Australia) where the stitch structure of a fabric used in mass-produced designs created using a computer was held to be a work of artistic craftsmanship. This followed the approach of Lord Simon in Hensher.

It has been suggested that – possibly because of the lack of clear guidance in Hensher – few claims to works of artistic crafts-

71. As the works were made by seamstresses in India (to the designs of designers in England) they were held to be works of craftsmanship but, although pleasing to the eye, the works did not have sufficient artistry or creativity to qualify as 'artistic'.
72. To add further confusion, Uma Suthersanen, in her *Design Law in Europe* (London: Sweet & Maxwell, 2000) at 16-050, refers to an unreported case Hourahine v Everdell & Mitchard which concerned pop-up greetings cards. These were held to be works of craftsmanship (on the basis of the effort put into constructing the card) but were not artistic. Notwithstanding criticism of the Court of Appeal e.g. by Lord Reid (at 55), the Court of Appeal in Hensher was nevertheless relied on to the effect that for a work to qualify as a work of artistic craftsmanship its utilitarian or functional appeal should not be the primary inducement to its acquisition or retention (per Russell LJ at 49) and the functional aspect predominated in this case.
73. High Court 2 February 2001; Rimer J.
74. Transcript at page 52. Here the garments were prototypes for mass production and machine made; also Mrs Guild did not appear to intend creating a work of art or even regard herself as an artist; so they were not works of artistic craftsmanship.

manship have been raised in the courts.[75] A leading text, Laddie, strongly rejects any test which may involve a question of taste, subjective quality or personal opinion as it exceeds the functions of a court of law to adjudicate on these matters and they are inconsistent with the very concept of the rule of law.[76] To overcome this Laddie proposes a test essentially similar to that of Lord Reid in Hensher.[77]

CRITERIA FOR PROTECTION I.E. WORK MUST BE 'ORIGINAL'[78]

The standard required for a work to qualify as 'original' is very low. It does not mean the work is novel, inventive or unique. An often cited case is University of London Press Limited v University Tutorial Press Limited[79] which considered what was meant by 'original' in the context of a literary work. According to the judge:

> The word 'original' does not in this connection mean that the work must be the expression of original or inventive thought. Copyright Acts are not concerned with the originality of ideas but with the expression of thought, and, in the case of a 'literary work,' with the expression of thought in print or writing. The originality which is required relates to the expression of the thought. But the Act [Copyright Act 1911] does not require that the expres-

75. Laddie, Prescott, Vitoria et al., *The Modern Law of Copyright and Designs* (third edition, London: Butterworths, 2000) ('Laddie') at 4.31.
76. Laddie above at 4.30 citing a number of cases where the courts have refused to adjudicate on questions that are not susceptible of judicial determination including White v Mellin [1895] AC 154 at 165, HL per Lord Herschell (whether one trader's product was 'better' than another) and Harris v Warren and Phillips [1918] 35 RPC 217 at 221-222 per Eve J (relative merits of musical compositions and whether they constituted the mature art of their composers).
77. Craftsmanship is seen as the working of materials by manual dexterity to produce the work and 'artistic' relates to the visual appearance of the work which must be significant in that persons wish to acquire and keep the work on especial account of its appearance (Laddie at 4.30). Laddie sees such a two part test as the only one actually workable.
78. For a thorough examination of this difficult area see Bently and Sherman, pp. 80-98
79. [1916] 2 Ch 601.

sion must be in an original or novel form, but that the work must not be copied from another work – that it should originate from the author.[80]

It remains the case that some degree of skill and labour on the part of the author is required to qualify a work as 'original'[81] but no more than trivial effort and skill are required for these purposes.[82] Also what counts in the context of artistic works is whether the skill and labour applied to the new work pertains to that which is visually significant: this is particularly important when the work is derived from another work (a so-called 'derivative work'): mere 'slavish' copying, even if it involves considerable skill, labour or judgment cannot confer originality.[83] In cases of copying from another work there needs to be some element of material alteration or embellishment which suffices to make the totality of the work an original work.[84] Indeed the au-

80. Per Peterson J at 608-609. The judgement also appears to acknowledge what is often called the idea-expression dichotomy in copyright: copyright does not protect ideas as such, but only their expression – see below.
81. Interlego A.G. v Tyco Industries [1989] 1 A.C. 217 at 262H.
82. Autospin (Oil Seals) v Beehive Spinning (a firm) [1995] RPC 683 at 694, cited in SPE International Ltd v Professional Preparation Contractors (UK) Ltd [2000] EIPR N-19. Certainly the level of originality in the UK appears lower than that required in the USA where following the Supreme Court in Feist Publications v Rural Telephone Service Co 499 US 340 (1991) 113 L Ed 358 (1991) the work must possess at least some minimal degree of creativity (at 369). In Europe the position is different still – not only must origination be present but the author's own personality must find its expression in the work. Also attempts at harmonisation by the European Commission (e.g. in the context of the Term Directive (93/98/EEC of 29 October 1993, OJ L 290/9 (24 November 1993) where the concept of originality is applied to computer programs, databases and photographs) speak of 'the author's own intellectual creation reflecting his personality' as the criterion for protection (see Art 6 and Recital 17 of the Term Directive). See generally Stanley Lai, *The Copyright Protection of Computer Software in the United Kingdom* (Oxford: Hart Publishing, 2000) ('Lai') at 2.6-2.14.
83. Interlego AG v Tyco Industries and Others [1989] 1 AC 217 at 262H as cited e.g. in SPE International Ltd v Professional Preparation Contractors (UK) Ltd Chancery Division, High Court, 15 July 1999, Rimer J; [2000] EIPR N-19.
84. Interlego v Tyco at 263C. It must be stressed that using existing material as the basis for a new work will not necessarily prevent the new work

dience to which the artistic work is addressed appears relevant: certainly in cases involving engineering drawings what counts is whether the new work is visually significant to an engineer, not a layman.[85]

Given the low standard required for 'originality,' this hurdle to copyright protection in the UK is likely to be satisfied for most artistic works, including such relatively 'unoriginal' works as photographs of paintings or objects in a gallery's collection.[86] Nevertheless mere mechanical copying will not be sufficient to confer 'originality': in The Reject Shop plc v Manners[87] the Court of Appeal rejected an argument that a slightly enlarged image made by a photocopier was itself an original artistic work: there was no skill and labour involved in the copying sufficient to confer 'originality of an artistic character'.[88]

THE NEED FOR FIXATION/PERMANENCE OF THE WORK?

In the case of a literary, dramatic or musical work, copyright will only subsist in the work if it is recorded in writing or otherwise.[89] There are no equivalent provisions for artistic works, although it is arguable that a similar requirement may be demanded by the courts for artistic works. Indeed on public policy grounds it can be argued that as copyright is in the nature of a monopoly there must be certainty in its subject matter to avoid injustice.[90] Cer-

benefiting from copyright protection – original thought is not required for 'originality,' although the law will protect against plagiarism of a work in copyright (see for example Andrew Christoffer v Poseidon Film Distributors Ltd [2000] E.I.P.R. N-34 (here the source of the copyright work was Homer's Odyssey)).

85. Billhöfer Maschinenfabrik GmSH v T.H. Dixon and Co. Ltd [1990] FSR 105.
86. See the section on photographs above.
87. [1995] FSR 870.
88. Per Legatt LJ at 876.
89. S3(2) CDPA.
90. By Farwell LJ in Tate v Fullbrook [1908] 1 KB 821 at 822-833. This case concerned infringement of a dramatic work (music hall 'dramatic sketch'). The question arose whether scenic effects, stage 'business' and the make up of the actors were protected by copyright. They were held not to be as they could not be the subject of printing and publication, and in any event the scope of the monopoly granted by copyright had

tainly some element of fixation has on occasion been found necessary for artistic works in UK law. For example, in addition to the 'Adam Ant' case (Merchandising Corp. of America v Harpbond[91]) noted earlier in the context of defining a 'painting' for copyright purposes, in the Australian case Komesaroff v Mickle and Others[92] works of 'kinetic art' ('sand pictures') were found to lack sufficient permanence to be classed as works of artistic craftsmanship[93]: no sand picture was static for any length of time. In Davis (J&S) (Holdings) Ltd v Wright Health Group Ltd[94] Whitford J. held that the models and casts in that case were not sculptures as inter alia it was never intended they should have any continuing existence.[95] In Creation Records (discussed above in the contact of Collages) an assembly of *objets trouvés* was inter alia not a collage as it was intrinsically ephemeral, existing for only a few hours.[96] However the general proposition that something which has a mere transient existence cannot be a 'work of sculpture' was rejected by Laddie J in Metix (UK) Limited v G.H. Maughan (Plastics) Limited.[97] So the position is unclear.

to be clear. Farwell LJ's dictum was approved by the Privy Council in Green v Broadcasting Corporation of New Zealand [1989] 2 All ER 1056 at 1058 (dramatic 'format' of the TV show 'Opportunity Knocks' inter alia not certain enough to be protected by copyright e.g. identity of performers would change from show to show, the material presented would change; nor was it a dramatic work as the format lacked the essential characteristic of having sufficient unity to be capable of performance). See also Laddie at 3.33.

91. [1983] FSR 32.
92. [1988] RPC 204 at 210.
93. At 210.
94. [1988] RPC 403.
95. This case concerned plastic dental impression plates – the items in question were stages in producing these items rather than independent artistic works, so Whitford J's decision at 410-412 is not surprising. See also the comments of Lord Simon in Hensher noted above.
96. Whether or not there was artistic intent in the creation of the assembly was held to be irrelevant.
97. [1997] FSR 718. It was accepted in an argument before Laddie J that a sculpture made from ice is no less a sculpture because it may melt as soon as the temperature rises.

THE IDEA/EXPRESSION DICHOTOMY

It is also important to bear in mind the so-called 'idea/expression dichotomy' in copyright law when seeking to determine the scope of protection for artistic works.[98] Simply put, copyright does not protect ideas, only the form in which they are expressed. As Lord Salmon once put it: 'it is trite law that there can be no copyright in an idea.'[99] So for example, no one could copyright pointillism as an artistic style, but Seurat's paintings (if in copyright) would themselves be protected from copying as original artistic works. This dichotomy appears in copyright infringement cases from time to time where the style, technique or other elements of a design or painting have been reproduced but there has been no

98. Not all authors admit the existence of such a 'dichotomy' in UK law, which has no express statutory basis – Laddie calls it the 'idea/expression fallacy' (see Laddie at 3.74) but it nevertheless appears in copyright cases on a regular basis (a few examples include per Nichols LJ in ENTEC (Pollution Control) Ltd v Abacus Mouldings [1992] FSR 332, George Ward (Moxley) Ltd v Richard Sankey Ltd and Another [1988] FSR 66, Bradbury, Agnew & Co v Day (1916) 32 TLR 349). In any event, as Lord Hoffmann recently observed in his exposition of the dichotomy in Designers Guild v Russell Williams [2000] 1 WLR 2416 at 2422 (HL), the distinction does find a place in the Agreement on the Trade-Related Aspects of Intellectual Property (TRIPS) (O.J. 1994 L.336, p.213) to which the UK is a party (in article 9.2). It is therefore submitted that this distinction is a useful and necessary starting point when considering if there has been infringement of an artistic work. Certainly it must be used with care, as Lord Hailsham commented (citing Professor Joad of 'Brains Trust' fame) 'it all depends on what you mean by ideas' (L.B. (Plastics) Limited v Swish Products Limited [1979] RPC 551 at 629 (HL), which Lord Hoffmann also referred to in Designers Guild (at 2422)). Laddie in any event is prepared to restate the principle on the basis that whilst there is no copyright in general ideas, an original combination of ideas may constitute a substantial part of a copyright work (at 4.43) (citing Lord Hailsham in Swish Products (at 629) (see above), and Astbury J in Austin v Columbia Gramaphone Co [1917-23] MCC 398 at 408 and again in Vane v Famous Players Film Co Ltd [1923-28] MCC 374 at 398).

99. L.B. (Plastics) Limited v Swish Products Limited [1979] RPC 551 at 633 (HL). For a discussion of how the UK and USA have developed and applied this principle with emphasis on software copyright see Lai n. 85 above.

literal copying.[100] It is then frequently necessary to determine whether what has been copied is (protected) expression or merely an idea not eligible for copyright protection.

FITTING MODERN ART INTO THE CATEGORY OF 'ARTISTIC WORKS' UNDER THE CDPA[101]

The copyright protection afforded to a variety of modern and contemporary art is a matter of some debate. Often such works either strain to fall within any category of 'artistic work' under the CDPA or even if they appear to fall within a specific category their protection is uncertain as they may not be 'original'.

In an attempt to pull together the various strands of this first section of this paper what follows is a discussion of the copyright protection UK law might give various twentieth century art forms, assuming that the artist is either alive or died less than 70 years ago.

(a) Ready-mades, objets trouvés and assemblage[102]

In this art form the artist elevates ordinary objects to the status of art, challenging accepted ideas about what art is. Marcel Duchamp's exhibition in 1913 of a bicycle wheel attached to a stool and signed by the artist is the first so-called 'ready-made'. The everyday, 'found object' or '*objet trouvé*', used as the ready-made may also be used as part of an assemblage (see below).

Ready-mades would have to fall within the definition of 'sculpture' under the CDPA in order to be protected by copyright as 'artistic works.' As discussed above, UK law defines sculpture very broadly. But even if considered as 'sculpture', are such works original? Here the originality consists in taking the found object out of its usual setting and exhibiting it in an artistic context. If the object was created with an artistic purpose in

100. See for example, per Morritt LJ and Lord Hoffmann in Designers Guild v Russell Williams discussed below.
101. For a discussion of the position internationally, see Bently and Sherman "Copyright Aspects of Art Loans' in Palmer (ed) *Art Loans* (London: Kluwer, 1996)
102. The definitions of these terms are derived from the Glossary in *The 20th Century Art Book* (London: Phaidon Press, 1996)

mind then as noted earlier it can be argued the courts are more likely to protect the work.

In Creation Records Ltd. and others v. News Group Newspapers Ltd. (1997)[103] it was argued by counsel for the plaintiffs that Carl Andre's famous brick 'sculpture'[104] ought to benefit from copyright protection. Whilst this point was not developed further by the judge, the 'permanence' of such works was distinguished from the transitory assembly of found objects that formed the disputed matter of this case: the latter did not qualify for protection either as a sculpture or as a collage. In any event recent cases discussed above (in particular Metix v Maughan[105]) suggest the courts are more willing to look at the intention and status (as 'artist') of the creator when deciding to class a work as a 'sculpture'.

Where a number of found objects are brought together to form a work on canvas, such as Arman's Crusaders, in which stacks of paint brushes are assembled and stuck together to form the work, then an 'assemblage' is created. It is suggested that where the assemblage consists of items affixed to canvas then, following the definition of collage put forward by Lloyd J in Creation Records,[106] such works are likely to be protected as collages under UK law.

(b) Appropriation Art[107]

Here the artist expressly sets out to 'borrow' images from other sources and to include or assimilatethem into their own work.

103. 16 Tr L544, The Times 29 April 1997 – discussed above.
104. Equivalent VIII (1966), controversially acquired and displayed by the Tate Gallery.
105. [1997] FSR 718.
106. 'In my view a collage does indeed involve as an essential element the sticking of two or more things together'.
107. See Brad Sherman, 'Appropriating the Postmodern: Copyright and the Challenge of the New' (1995) 4 *Social & Legal Studies* 31 ('Sherman') for a discussion of this area. Sherman lists examples of appropriation art as including Mike Bildo's full size copies of paintings by Cezanne, Matisse, Pollock, Lichtenstein and Picasso (to which Bildo attaches his signature and renames them) and Marcel Duchamp's addition of a moustache to a copy of the Mona Lisa (at 32). Jeff Koons' well known appropriation of the 'String of Puppies' photograph, the

Whilst this practice can be traced to Dadaism, Surrealism and Pop art,[108] 'appropriation art' is rooted in postmodernism.[109] It can therefore be debated as to whether appropriation art is sufficiently original, as here the expressive form (as opposed to merely the idea) of the original work is copied. In addition the appropriation artist can herself be vulnerable to a charge of plagiarism, or of copyright infringement.

It is worthwhile citing the Privy Council in Interlego v Tyco as to what is necessary to afford copyright protection to a copy of a work: '[t]here must in addition be some element of material alteration or embellishment which suffices to make the totality of the work an original work.'[110] In the context of artistic works such alteration or embellishment must be 'visually significant'.[111] It is not enough that what is done conveys 'information'[112] – so although in the process of appropriation the meaning of the work is changed by placing it in a new context, its visual signifi-

subject of the US case Rogers v Koons 960 F.2d 301 is another example.

108. Sherman at 32 (citing A. Bonnett, 'Art, Ideology and Everyday Space: Subversive Tendencies from Dada to Postmodernism' (1992) 10 *Society and Space* 69).
109. 'Reappropriating existing representations that are effective precisely because they are loaded with pre-existing meaning and putting them into new and ironic contexts is a typical form of postmodern...critique' (Linda Hutcheon, commenting on postmodern photography including the work of Cindy Sherman, Sherrie Levine and Martha Rosler, in her book *The Politics of Postmodernism* (London: Routledge, 1989) at 44). See also Sherman: '[b]y placing a well-known object such as the American flag, a painting by Picasso or an advertising logo in a new context, the appropriation artist aims to denaturalize it and thus to provide the borrowed object with a new meaning or vocabulary' (at 32).
110. Per Lord Oliver in Interlego AG v Tyco Industries Inc and others [1988] 3 All ER 949 at 972.
111. See discussion of 'originality' above.
112. This is properly the subject of literary works in copyright law (see Exxon v Exxon Insurance [1982] RPC 69) (see Sherman at 49 n.22).

cance may well not be. Hence it may not benefit from copyright protection.[113]

(c) Minimalist Art

'Minimalist art is [art] pared down to its essentials.'[114] Do such works embody sufficient original effort to be protected by copyright? UK law has afforded copyright protection to a variety of simple drawings, including a hand for a voting card[115], as discussed above, so it is submitted that copyright protection ought not to be a problem for most minimalist paintings and drawings. However the scope of protection will be very limited.

Indeed in a recent decision, Mr Justice Rimer, when considering the copyright protection in engineering manufacturing drawings for a mobile blast cleaning machine, concluded that an argument that the skill and effort in producing the drawing in question was too trivial to justify a claim of originality was one easy to advance but which he was not willing to accept. The judge quoted from the essay entitled 'Prose and Dr Tillotson' by Somerset Maugham, in which Maugham talked about an unforgettable and haunting picture by Mondrian consisting of some black lines and a red one on a white background and suggested that any viewer might think he could easily produce the work himself as it looked so simple. Maugham ended his essay by challenging the reader to try.[116]

(d) Modern Art and Advertising
– Gillian Wearing, Mehdi Norowzian and beyond

Some of the most creative British artists of recent times have abandoned or radically modified the use of traditional artistic media. Gillian Wearing, winner of the 1997 Turner Prize, is one of the best known of the so-called YBAs (Young British Artists).

113. See Sherman at 38-40. See also per Lord Oliver in Interlego AG v Tyco Industries Inc and others [1988] 3 All ER 949: 'essentially artistic copyright is concerned with the visual image' (at 972).
114. *20th Century Art Book*, Glossary (see n.105 above).
115. Kenrick v Lawrence (1890) 25 QBD 93
116. SPE International Ltd v Professional Preparation Contractors (UK) Ltd [2000] EIPR N-19; transcript at page 20.

A number of her works have also provided inspiration for advertising campaigns. For example, Signs (1993), a photographic work, where people on the street were asked by the artist to write down what they were feeling at the time on a sign they would then hold up in front of the camera (a well known one being of a young businessman with a sign reading 'I'm Desperate') inspired a Volkswagen advert. The advert showed a security guard, a harassed mother and others holding up signs that state what they are supposed to be feeling ('Sensitive' in the case of the security guard, 'Sex Chocolate Sex Chocolate' in the case of the mother). 2 into 1, where the voices of mother and sons are transposed, was emulated in a computer game advert. The artist protested about the taking of her ideas considering it to be 'theft', especially as there was no reference to her work.[117] But no court proceedings ensued (or at least have been reported).

A more recent copyright case, Norowzian v Arks Limited & others (No.2)[118] which went as far as the Court of Appeal, expressly considered the copyright protection afforded to contemporary artistic works, in this case a short film, *Joy*, created using 'jump cutting' editing techniques to give a surreal quality to the action of a man dancing to music. It was alleged by the director of *Joy*, Mr Norowzian, that Guinness infringed his copyright in Joy by making a very successful advert in a similar style. Called Anticipation, it portrayed a man who waits for his pint of Guinness to settle by carrying out a series of dancing movements to music with no dialogue. There were two characters (drinker and barman) and a similar jump cutting technique to that used in Joy was applied to the film with a similar result: the dancing man appears to indulge in a series of jerky movements that could not be achieved by a dancer in continous motion.[119]

Mr Norowzian failed both at interlocutory stage, full trial and on appeal to protect his copyright in Joy. At the interlocutory

117. For background on Gillian Wearing and the works of art discussed see Daring Wearing by Miranda Sawyer (an interview with the artist), *The Observer Magazine* 3 September 2000

118. [1998] FSR 394 (Steinfeld J. – interlocutory judgement); [1999] FSR 79 (Rattee J); [2000] FSR 363 (CA)

119. At 81

stage it was held that film copyright only protects the individual frames of a film from copying, which was not the case here. At full trial Rattee J dismissed an argument that Joy was a dramatic work on the grounds it was not capable of being physically performed. The Court of Appeal however held that a film could be a dramatic work but here there was no copyright infringement.[120] The idea/expression dichotomy was relevant: merely copying a style or technique was not copyright infringement.[121]

(e) Categories of 'Art' and the subsistence of copyright: some concluding thoughts

The confining definition of 'artistic works' in section 4(1) of the CDPA means the courts are increasingly having to determine whether works outside the boundaries of traditional art forms are protected by copyright.[122] In determining the subsistence of copyright, issues such as the fixation/permanence of the work, its

120. See for example Nourse LJ: 'As [Rattee J] recognised, the highest that can be put in favour of [Mr Norowzian] is that there is a striking similarity between the filming and editing styles and techniques used by the respective directors of the two films. But no copyright subsists in mere style or technique. [Counsel for the defendant Arks Ltd] instanced the technique of pointillism, which was originated by the neo-impressionists Seurat and Signac. That was a telling example. If, on seeing La Baignade, Asnieres at the Salon des Artistes Independents in 1884, another artist had used precisely the same technique in painting a scene in Provence, Seurat would have been unable, by the canons of English copyright law, to maintain an action against him. Other examples of original artistic styles or techniques whose imitation in the production of an entirely different subject matter would not found such an action might be the 'sprung rhythm' of Gerard Manley Hopkins' verse or the thematic build-up of Sibelius's second symphony. So here, the subject matter of the two films being, as [Rattee J] said, very different one from the other, the similarities of style and technique are insufficient to give [Mr Norowzian] a cause of action against the defendants.'

121. Because of the difficulties of sustaining a copyright infringement claim in such cases often a claim in passing off is pleaded but in the absence of an actionable misrepresentation this will fail. See Stokes, chapter eight.

122. See Creation Records v News Group Newspapers [1997] EMLR 444; Norowzian v Arks [2000] FSR 363 and other cases discussed above.

categorisation as a 'graphic work', 'sculpture', 'collage', 'film', 'dramatic work' etc, and its originality will arise.

In seeking to classify works within a specific category of 'artistic work' it is clear from section 4 of the CDPA that, except for 'works of artistic craftsmanship',[123] 'artistic quality' should not be a relevant factor. Nevertheless there have been occasions when the court cannot easily fit a work into a specific category; issues such as the intention of the creator and their status (as an 'artist') have been considered, despite both the specific language of section 4 and the often-expressed reluctance of the courts to determine questions of aesthetics.[124]

'Works of artistic craftsmanship' remains an ill-defined category of work. Various tests have been used to determine whether a work falls within this category.[125] These include considerations of the function of the work, the intention of the designer, whether the work appeals to the aesthetic senses, whether the designer is an artist-craftsman, whether the work is artistic or creative enough, that 'works of artistic craftsmanship' be given its ordinary and natural meaning, and so on. Given the increasing importance of 'craft' in artistic circles and the difficulties surrounding the protection of works as diverse as fashion designs, film sets, and patchwork bedspreads,[126] it is submitted that

123. Also (arguably) for works of architecture (see above).

124. See Metix (UK) v G.H. Maughan (Plastics) [1997] FSR 718: sculpture defined as 'a three dimensional work made by an artist's hand.' In considering whether the plastic moulds concerned were 'sculptures' Laddie J noted that their designers did not consider themselves to be 'artists' when they designed the moulds (nor would anyone else have considered them to be) and their only consideration in making the moulds was to achieve functional, as opposed to aesthetic, features. However artistic intent alone may not help if there is no fixation (see above and also per Lloyd J in Creation Records v News Group Newspapers [1997] EMLR 444 at 450, discussed above). Contrast Hi-Tech Autoparts [2002] F.S.R 15.

125. As discussed above.

126. See respectively Radley Gowns Ltd v Costas Spyrou [1975] FSR 455, Shelley Films Limited v Rex Features Limited [1994] EMLR 134, and Vermaat v Boncrest Ltd (The Times 23 June 2000; [2000] EIPR N-151; [2001] FSR 5; Intellectual Property Lawyer, Issue 3, July 2000 (at 10).

a clear and consistent approach by the courts is necessary in this area.[127]

Moving on from the category of work, the issue of 'fixation' remains a difficult one for artistic works. There is no statutory requirement of fixation for artistic works, and whether a work is intended to have a long or short existence should be irrelevant. However the cases on this issue appear to conflict. It is submitted that some element of fixation is surely necessary to define the scope of what is protected by copyright.[128] In practice, when considering whether the work in question is an 'artistic work' the issue of fixation will be dealt with: the very categories of 'artistic works' (graphic works, photographs, sculptures and collages) would seem to require such a determination.[129]

Originality as a necessary requirement for copyright remains wedded to the notion of 'sweat of the brow.' Xerographic or similar reproductions apart, skill and labour devoted to the visual expression of an artistic work will be sufficient to satisfy the threshold of 'originality' in UK law; 'creativity' finds no part in UK copyright law.[130] However, as Lord Hoffmann recently noted, 'copyright law protects foxes better than hedgehogs,'[131] so whilst a simple artistic work may be protected by copyright, the protection afforded to the artist to prevent copying may well be limited.[132]

127. Of course the whole area illustrates the various judicial approaches that can be taken to defining art and craft.
128. See for example Tate v Fullbrook [1908] 1 KB 821, discussed above.
129. See for example Creation Records v News Group Newspapers [1997] EMLR 444 discussed above, where the collocation of random unfixed objects was not a collage even if done with artistic intent.
130. Although this may gradually change in the light of EU copyright harmonisation as noted above: for example, the Term Directive (Directive 93/98/EEC) states that 'photographs which are original in the sense that they are the author's own intellectual creation shall be protected in accordance with Article 1 [extension of duration of copyright term to life plus 70 years] [emphasis added]. No other criteria shall be applied to determine their eligibility for protection. Member states may provide for the protection of other photographs.'
131. Designers Guild v Russell Williams (Textiles) Ltd [2000] 1 WLR 2416 at 2423E discussed below.
132. See Kenrick v Lawrence (1890) 25 QBD 93, discussed above.

In conclusion, how valid is the criticism that UK law is inflexible in its categorisation of artistic works? Do various forms of contemporary art fall outside the ambit of copyright? It is submitted that whilst clarity would be helpful in certain areas (most notably for works of artistic craftsmanship), in light of recent cases the categories of protected work in section 4 of the CDPA appear to have a reasonable degree of flexibility in practice.[133] One might argue that this reflects the pragmatic approach of the UK courts to copyright matters.

Art, Authorship and Digitisation

'Authorship' is central to copyright law. It is the author who creates the original work, something distinctive and worthy of special protection under copyright law.[134] Indeed it can be argued, as a leading scholar Peter Jaszi does, that the Romantic conception of authorship, 'the Wordsworthian vision of the 'author-genius' with privileged access to the numinous' continues to have abiding influence whether what is created is a Bach fugue, a Picasso or a piece of software.[135] The fact that this is often rhetorical, as when large corporations argue for the stronger protection of authors' rights (which of course their authors will be

133. For example there will generally be skill and labour expended in creating a ready-made and, following Metix (UK) v G.H. Maughan (Plastics) [1997] FSR 718, it is difficult to see why such a work cannot be classed as 'sculpture'. Of course in Creation Records v News Group Newspapers [1997] EMLR 444 the 'assemblage' concerned was denied copyright protection but here (following Metix v Maughan) the purpose of the work was surely central – if it had been created, not to be photographed for a clear commercial purpose and then immediately dismantled, but as a temporary installation to be exhibited, it is submitted a court would probably find some way of protecting the work.
134. Mark Poster, *What's the Matter with the Internet?* (Minneapolis: University of Minnesota Press, 2001) at 86.
135. Jaszi, 'Towards a Theory of Copyright: The Metamorphoses of 'Authorship' (1991) Duke Law Journal 455, at 459 (referring to Woodmansee, 'The Genius and the Copyright: Economic and Legal Conditions of the Emergence of the 'Author' 17 *Eighteenth-Century Stud* 425 (1983-1984)).

assigning to them anyway for relatively little, if any, consideration), in no way diminishes the importance of the author.

Certainly UK copyright law is rooted in the concept of the author, the person (artist, engraver, etc) who creates the 'work' in which copyright subsists.[136] Except in very limited circumstances (the work was computer-generated (even here the law constructs an 'author'[137]) or the author is 'unknown') all artistic works will have an author who is living or dead. The author will also be the first owner of copyright in the work unless it is made in the course of the author's employment or it is subject to Crown or some other governmental copyright.[138] The duration of copyright in a work is linked to the author's life and death, and only authors have moral rights in their works; they may also have an unwaivable right to remuneration from certain copies of their works.[139] The status of the author (e.g. their domicile) is also relevant to whether a work qualifies for copyright.

The law only recognises joint authorship in limited circumstances – where a work is produced by the collaboration of two or more authors in which the contribution of each author is not distinct from that of the other author or authors.[140] For example a work by the British artists Gilbert and George would be one of joint authorship.

Copyright law is therefore at variance with the postmodernist tendency to downplay the author, to view authors' creations as 'a fabric of quotations, resulting from a thousand sources of culture'.[141] Digitisation and the Internet also facilitate the death of a single author and encourage collaborative creations as well as

136. Section 9(1) CDPA
137. The person by whom the arrangements necessary for the creation of the work are undertaken (Section 9(3) CDPA). This harks back to the nineteenth century test for who the 'author' of a photograph was – it was the person who was the 'cause' of the picture which is produced (Nottage v Jackson (1883))
138. Section 11 CDPA
139. Article 4, Directive 92/100/EC
140. Section 10 CDPA
141. The quotation is from Roland Barthes' essay 'The Death of the Author' (1968) and cited in Stuart Sim (ed), *The Routledge Companion to Postmodernism* (London: Routledge, 2001), pp. 191-193.

the ready appropriation of images in digital form. The focus on the single identifiable author against whom 'originality' is assessed also poses problems for works of communal origin, for example aboriginal art.[142]

Yet copyright shows no sign of jettisoning the author. The law is therefore at variance with certain current artistic trends, some of which are discussed below.

Appropriation Versus Infringement

'The world is filled to suffocating. Man has placed his token on every stone. Every word, every image is leased and mortgaged. ... Succeeding the painter, the plagiarist no longer bears within him passions, humours, feelings, impressions, but rather this immense encyclopaedia from which he draws.' (Sherrie Levine, 'Statement')[143]

All creative effort is in a sense derivative. 'We stand on the shoulders of the scientists, artists and craftsmen who proceeded us. We borrow and develop what they have done; not necessarily as parasites, but simply as the next generation. It is at the heart of what we know by progress.'[144] Appropriation art was discussed earlier in the context of whether these sorts of artistic works are protected by copyright in their own right. Of greater concern to appropriation artists such as Sherrie Levine is the extent to which they may have infringed copyright in creating their works.

Under English law the copyright owner has a bundle of exclusive rights which he can prevent others from exercising. These so-called 'restricted acts' include:[145]

142. See for example Yumbulul v Reserve Bank of Australia (1991) IPR 481 – 'Australia's copyright law does not provide adequate recognition of Aboriginal community claims to regulate the reproduction and use of works which are essentially communal in origin' (at 490).
143. In Harrison and Wood (eds) *Art in Theory: 1900-1992* (Oxford: Blackwell, 1992) at 1067).
144. Mr Justice Laddie, 'Copyright: Over-strength, Over-regulated, Overrated?'[1996] 5 EIPR 253 at 259.
145. S16 CDPA.

1. the right to copy[146] the work (this includes (in respect of an artistic work) making a two dimensional copy of a three dimensional work, and vice versa), and
2. the right to issue copies to the public.

Copyright in a work is infringed by a person who, without the licence of the copyright owner, does, or authorises another to do, any of the acts restricted by copyright.

For there to be copyright infringement, the copying must involve the copying of the work as a whole or a substantial part of it, and either directly or indirectly.[147] The definition of what is meant by 'a substantial part' is not a precise one:, there is no one test and the phrase is susceptible to a number of meanings.[148] A recent attempt to define what substantial means in the context of the CDPA was made in The Newspaper Licensing Agency v Marks and Spencer Plc[149] where Gibson LJ was of the view that the word described something more than de minimis, something considerable in amount sufficient to make it worthy of consideration.[150]

In assessing whether there has been copying of the whole or a substantial part of the work it will probably be necessary to give

146. Copying in relation to a work means reproducing the work in any material form. This includes storing the work in any medium by electronic means (s.17(2)).
147. S13(3) CDPA.
148. S16(2) CDPA. The test of 'substantial' is of quality not quantity (see Ladbroke (Football) v Hill (William) (Football) [1964] 1 WLR 273). See Bauman v Fussell [1978] RPC 485 (CA) (painting derived from a photograph did not infringe the photograph – see in particular the dissenting judgement of Romer LJ) and Krisarts v Briarfine [1977] FSR 577 (interlocutory judgement: plaintiffs had an arguable case of copyright infringement where the defendants used paintings in which the plaintiffs held copyright to assist them in producing their own paintings of well-known views of London which were not slavish copies of the plaintiffs' copyright works) for some specific examples of how the courts have dealt with the copying of art. Infringing copyright may give rise to a civil liability (payment of damages to the aggrieved copyright owner, granting of an injunction and delivery up to prevent the infringement) as well as a possible criminal liability – see Chapter VI, CDPA.
149. [2000] 3 WLR 1256.
150. At 1265G.

some consideration to the 'originality' of what has been copied. This is because UK copyright law seeks to protect the skill and labour of the artist and so the originality of what is copied cannot be ignored. In what is currently the leading artistic copyright case Lord Hoffmann said:

> Generally speaking in cases of artistic copyright, the more abstract and simple the copied idea, the less likely it is to constitute a substantial part. Originality, in the sense of the author's skill and labour, tends to lie in the detail with which the basic idea is presented. Copyright law protects foxes better than hedgehogs.[151]

So where the idea copied is trivial or commonplace there is likely to be no infringement; after that it is a matter of degree. In any event the dominant rationales underpinning UK copyright law must be borne in mind. These are that copyright law seeks to protect the skill and labour of the artist and also that it is unjust to reap where you have not sown. For example in the leading case involving artistic works, Designers Guild Limited v Russell Williams (Textiles) Limited[152] the House of Lords stated: '[t]he law of copyright rests on a very clear principle: that anyone who by his or her own skill and labour creates an original work of whatever character shall, for a limited period, enjoy an exclusive right to copy that work. No one else may for a season reap what the copyright owner has sown.'[153] Also it was stated that the test for infringement was 'did [the allegedly infringing work] incorporate a substantial part of the skill and labour expended by the designer of [the copied work] in producing [the copied work]?'[154]

151. Designers Guild Ltd v Russell Williams (Textiles) Ltd [2000] 1 W.L.R. 2416 at 2423. The quotation is apparently to the Greek poet Archilochus: 'The fox knows many things, but the hedgehog knows one big thing' made famous by Sir Isaiah Berlin's 1953 essay 'The Hedgehog and the Fox' which discusses the tension between monist and pluralist visions of the world and history – see Gillian Haggart, Book Review (Simon Stokes – 'Art & Copyright'), [2002] E.I.P.R. 384.
152. [2000] 1 WLR 2416.
153. Per Lord Bingham of Cornhill at 2418A.
154. Per Lord Scott of Foscote: he spoke approvingly of the test proposed in the second edition of Laddie (pp 92/93, para 2-108) where in-

What is clear is that UK law has no general fair use defence to copyright infringement but only a limited number of 'fair dealing' defences. Unlike some countries there is no 'parody' defence. The use of a work in a different context will still be infringement if all or a substantial part of the protected work is taken, harsh though this may be to some artists. So post-modern tendencies towards parody or appropriation can potentially fall foul of the law.

Consider for example the controversy late in 2000 in the UK surrounding Glenn Brown's Turner Prize entry "The Loves of Shepherds 2000' (more properly entitled "The Loves of Shepherds (After Tony Roberts) 2000'). This brought into public debate the issue of when does 'inspiration' or 'appropriation' amount to copyright infringement? In the case of Loves of Shepherds 2000 there would in the author's view appear little doubt that Glenn Brown's 'copy' of Anthony Roberts's book jacket illustration for the Robert A. Heinlein novel Double Star is a clear case of copyright infringement (although Glenn Brown's lawyer Stuart Lockyear has argued fair dealing for the purposes of criticism or review ought to apply). Nevertheless a number of art critics were quoted as saying that in The Loves of Shepherds Glenn Brown, although obviously 'inspired' by the book jacket illustration, had used considerable skill and creativity to produce his work. Indeed Glenn Brown was quoted by The Times at the time as saying, 'I have radically altered Roberts's work in terms of scale and colour.' This highlights the different approaches that can be taken to appropriation and the conflicts that can in UK law arise when artists insist on their legal rights when appropriation has occurred.

It is worth looking into parody in more detail. Parody is a word with a wide range of meanings and appropriation may or

fringement of copyright by an altered copy is concerned (this was the case here) '[h]as the infringer incorporated a substantial part of the independent skill, labour etc contributed by the original author in creating the copyright work?' Lord Scott considered this a useful test 'based as it is on an underlying principle of copyright law, namely, that a copier is not at liberty to appropriate the benefit of another's skill and labour' (at 2431G).

may not involve parody. Parody may include an element of satire or ridicule and in more general terms the work parodied is effectively re-used in all or part to perform a different function than the original work. However unlike plagiarism, where the intention is to conceal the derivation of the work copied, the parodist needs to rely on the audience's awareness of the target work or genre to be successful – 'the complicity of the audience is the sine qua non of its enjoyment'.[155] A leading author on the subject, Linda Hutcheon, has spoken of parody as 'imitation characterised by ironic inversion, not always at the expense of the parodied text'.[156] As well as copyright and moral rights, other intellectual property rights not the subject of this paper including trade mark law may also protect against parody.

The parodist is unlikely to face problems if only the style or genre of other works is made the subject of parody for there is then unlikely to be copyright infringement. However where the expression, as opposed to the mere idea, of a work is copied for the purposes of parody then there may well be an issue. As noted above, UK law, unlike Spanish,[157] Belgian[158] and French[159] law, makes no express exceptions for parody. A parody will constitute an infringement of copyright if the parodist has taken a substantial part of the protected work, although merely 'conjuring up' the work being parodied will not normally amount to infringement.[160]

155. Gredley and Maniatis 'Parody : A Fatal Attraction: Part 1 : the Nature of Parody and its Treatment in Copyright (1997) 7 EIPR 339.
156. Linda Hutcheon, *A Theory of Parody: The Teaching of Twentieth-Century Art Forms* (London: Methuen, 1985) ('Hutcheon') at 6. See also her later work, *The Politics of Postmodernism* (London: Routledge, 1989).
157. Real decreto legislativo, 12 abril 1996, Num. 1/1996, Propriedad Intelectual, Art. 39.
158. Loi de 30 juin 1994 relative au droit d'auteur et aux driot voisins, Art. 22.
159. Loi de juillet 1992 relative au code de la propriete intellectuelle Article 112-5. Note that Directive 2001/29/EC on the harmonization of certain aspects of copyright and related rights in the information society will permit Member States to allow exceptions in their copyright laws to permit 'use for the purpose of caricature, parody or pastiche' (Article 3 (k)).
160. Section 16 CDPA: in Williamson Music Ltd v Pearson Partnership Ltd [1987] FSR 97 the test formulated by Judge Paul Baker QC was

Parodists also potentially face liability for infringement of moral rights – that of derogatory treatment and the right to object to false attribution of authorship.[161]

It is a matter of some debate as to when a parody might constitute derogatory treatment. Does the parody have to be offensive to the spirit of the work, or will most parodies not be derogatory treatment in any event. This is because they will not usually be prejudicial to the artist's honour or reputation as they will not be made out to be the work of the artist?[162] It is also possible that certain parodies may benefit from one of the 'fair dealing' defences under the CDPA, in particular fair dealing for the purposes of criticism or review.[163]

'whether the parody, on the one hand, conjures up the idea of the original work and no more than the idea or, on the other hand, whether it uses a substantial part of the expression of the original work' (at 107).

161. Under section 84(1) of the CDPA, which is actionable without proof of damage. See Alan Kenneth Mackenzie Clark v Associated Newspapers Ltd [1998] RPC 261 – this case involved a spoof diary of the politician Alan Clark by Peter Bradshaw entitled 'Alan Clark's Secret Political Diaries': the plaintiff succeeded under both section 84(1) and the law of passing off.

162. See e.g. Clark v Associated Newspapers Limited [1998] RPC 261 a case in which derogatory treatment did not arise as there was no 'treatment' of the plaintiff's work – the plaintiff's style rather than his actual work was involved.

163. Section 31: in Williamson Music v The Pearson Partnership Ltd Judge Paul Baker Q.C. seemed to accept that fair dealing for the purpose of criticism or review might be successfully relied on in certain circumstances but declined to discuss the matter further in this case (see Copinger on Copyright (London 2000) at 9-18). For a US approach to fair dealing/fair use consider the well-known US case Rogers v Koons (1992) 960 F 2d 301 where the celebrated kitsch artist Jeff Koons was unable to rely on the US fair use defence when sued for copyright infringement in respect of a sculpture he created. The sculpture was a copy of a well-known black and white photograph 'Puppies' showing a man and a woman on a bench with a string of eight German Shepherd puppies. Koons argued that he had created a parody of modern society. However the court were of the view that the work copied must itself be, at least in part, the object of parody – this was to set some practicable boundaries to this defence. The defendant's 'bad faith' and 'profit-making motives' were also fatal to his case. A similar result was also reached in United Feature Syndicate Inc v Koons 817 F. Supp.

In any event there remains a continuing debate about whether parody should be afforded special treatment under the law. According to the UK copyright scholar Michael Spence four arguments often advanced are:[164] (a) parody should be treated as a distinctive genre as it deserves special treatment; (b) the problem of parody is one of 'market failure' as owners of copyright works are unlikely to grant licenses to permit the creation of parodies and so the law should intervene to allow new creative works such as parodies to come into existence; (c) parody involves the 'transformative' use of a copyright work i.e. a new creative work arises which is not a market substitute for the earlier work notwithstanding its dependence on it; and (d) the parodist's right to free speech should be protected. In conclusion Spence considers that parody by itself does not require special legislation in the UK – existing statutes and laws potentially give judges the scope to balance the rights of intellectual property holders and the free speech rights of parodists.[165]

370 (S.D. N.Y. 1993) where Koons appropriated the Garfield Comic Strip character 'Odie' for his 'Banality Show'.

164. See Spence, "Intellectual Property and the Problem of Parody' (1998) 114 LQR 594 at 601-615.

165. At 615-620. In particular he refers to clause 3 of the Human Rights Bill as requiring the courts to interpret existing intellectual property statutes in a manner compatible with the right to free speech and to keep that right in view when fashioning remedies for intellectual property infringement. In fact Article 10(1) of the European Convention on Human Rights has been raised before the courts in the context of parody by Counsel for the Defendants in Alan Clark v Associated Newspapers Ltd [1998] RPC 261 at 269-270. Lightman J gave this argument short shrift, describing it as totally misconceived: there was no interference with the defendant's freedom of expression in this case (the right of the defendant to parody the works of the plaintiff was never in question and in any event Article 10(2) makes clear that the right is subject to the rights of others, in this case the right to object to false attribution of authorship).

APPROPRIATION AND PARODY: SOME CONCLUDING THOUGHTS

A leading US scholar Yen has eloquently pointed out[166] that striking a balance between the interests of authors and the public is crucial in setting the limits to which copyright law can be used to prevent appropriation. Yen stresses that authorship in its broadest sense is possible only when future authors are able to borrow from those who went before them. If too much of a work is reserved as private property through the copyright system then authors will find it impossible to create. A strong public domain is a vital part of any copyright system.

COPYLEFT[167]

If the need to appropriate, borrow or parody can potentially pose problems for artists, might one solution be to emulate the model for creation used in 'open source' or 'copyleft' software?[168] Here is an 'open to the world', unilateral licensing model where anyone is free to copy and reuse all or part of the original software code, as long as others also have the right to do the same to the newly created code. There is no reason why this model could not also be applied to artistic works. But it would be necessary to protect moral rights: to ensure each artist got proper credit and that there was redress against derogatory treatment.

166. Yen "The Interdisclipinary Future of Copyright Theory' in Woodmansee and Jaszi (eds), *The Construction of Authorship* (Durham: Duke UP, 1994), pp. 159-161.
167. For a useful analysis in the area of literary copyright see Andrew Stokes, 'Authorship, Collaboration and Copyright: A View from the UK'. [2002] ENT. L.R.123.
168. See www.gnu.org

In fact a "Free Art Licence' has already been devised.[169] The rationale behind the licence is set out in the Preamble to the licence:

> With this Free Art License, you are authorised to copy, distribute and freely transform the work of art while respecting the rights of the originator. Far from ignoring the author's rights, this license recognises them and protects them. It reformulates their principle while making it possible for the public to make creative use of the works of art. Whereas current literary and artistic property rights result in restriction of the public's access to works of art, the goal of the Free Art License is to encourage such access. The intention is to make work accessible and to authorise the use of its resources by the greatest number of people: to use it in order to increase its use, to create new conditions for creation in order to multiply the possibilities of creation, while respecting the originators in according them recognition and defending their moral rights. In fact, with the arrival of the digital age, the invention of the Internet and free software, a new approach to creation and production has made its appearance. It also encourages a continuation of the process of experimentation undertaken by many contemporary artists. Knowledge and creativity are resources which, to be true to themselves, must remain free, i.e. remain a fundamental search which is not directly related to a concrete application. Creating means discovering the unknown, means inventing a reality without any heed to realism. Thus, the object(ive) of art is not equivalent to the finished and defined art object. This is the basic aim of this Free Art License: to promote and protect artistic practice freed from the rules of the market economy.

For the Free Art Licence to fully succeed it needs an ever increasing community of artists to work within its terms. Of course where the artist seeks to appropriate commercial art or images outside the community of Free Art Licensees they will in any event be outside of the protection of the licence.

Conclusion

This paper has sought to explore the relationship between art and copyright in certain areas of UK copyright law. Art has no special treatment in UK copyright law. In every case except for a

169. See www.artlibre.org for more background. See also www.creativecommons.org and Simon Stokes, *Digital Copyright* (London: Butterworths, 2002).

'work of artistic craftsmanship', regardless of artistic quality, if the work embodies some original skill and labour and falls within one of the categories under the CDPA it will be protected. Similarly the scope of what is protected from infringement is also determined by reference to whether sufficient (i.e. a substantial part) of the skill and labour of the creator has been appropriated.

The concept of 'authorship' in UK law remains wedded to Romantic notions of the author/creator. Collaborative or group works or works based on appropriation fall less easily into the copyright system. In the words of one commentator 'the evaluation of authorship from a linear, modernist, single-author concept to a circular, post modern collective understanding is at the heart of the present copyright debate. ... the law frames copyright in modernist terms, not because it any longer is, but because it is expedient to proceed as if it still were'.[170]

As far as the author is aware, Copyleft and the 'free art licence' have made few inroads into UK artistic practice, challenging though this movement is. (www.free-art.org is one.) It is certainly a model that deserves to be better known in the visual arts.

Looking to the future, the European Union has not yet sought to fully harmonise the law of artistic copyright or harmonise moral rights. The recent Information Society Copyright Directive (Directive 2001/29/EC) does not oblige member states to harmonise their laws on fair use/fair dealing, other than by effectively eliminating certain current exceptions and constraining what exceptions states may include in their laws. This means that differences will remain, particularly between the common law/copyright approach of the UK and other EU states.

170. Karsten Schubert, review of Stokes, 'Art & Copyright', *Burlington Magazine*, February 2002 at 115.

Art and Copy – A Legal Historian's Reflections on Copyright

Ditlev Tamm[*]

Artistic creation does not necessarily involve the copying of other artists. Writing is not only about copying what others have written, though certain writing practices, such as that of lawyers, depend much on the explication and commentary of what has already been written. Art is not created out of thin air, nor can a text ever be entirely independent of what has already been written. Artists and writers tend to be deeply knowledgeable about their precursors; what might be called a debt is also known as inspiration.

Copyright establishes the limits to be imposed on the use of artworks, whether in the plastic arts or in writing, deemed worthy of protection. Copyright does not prevent one from doing what creative people have always done – to stand on the shoulders of giants. One is permitted to follow and modify ideas set forth by writers or artists, thinkers or researchers, more inventive than ourselves. But we may not merely copy them. This seems fair, and desirable. There is however an important and problematic distinction between artworks and ideas. An idea can be presented by someone other than its inventor, but the presentation of that idea must acknowledge the inventor. Copyright law protects only the specific form of a work: an idea rephrased in other words cannot be protected by copyright law. An idea

* Dr.jur. et phil., Professor of Law, University of Copenhagen

can be stolen, though the specific sequence of words with which that idea was first presented is protected. Although the law does not protect ideas as such, it is clearly unethical to pass off as one's own what one knows to be the work of another. Researchers can be happy that copyright does at least protect the form of words in which you have chosen to present your ideas.

The invention of copyright was a huge step in the protection of human inventiveness and creativity: authors and artists have gained much from this legal device. Copyright law is there not only to protect but even to stimulate creativity. It is broad enough to admit quotations and those quiet allusions to dead masters that make up the conversation of true inventiveness. Literature is both a conversation and a struggle between the living and the dead. What writer has not made use of Homer? And still this *agon* continues, unhampered by laws.

Copyright can however complicate a writer's life. In recent developments, rights have been extended for periods of increasing duration. A historian hoping to illustrate a book on events of the not-so-recent past finds himself having to undertake a cumbersome search for the identity of the person who took the photograph. This often proves impossible in practical terms, and one must resort to the device of asking anyone who holds the right to announce themselves. Such demands and devices do not encourage a proper respect for copyright. What ought to be a protection for creativity can become a device for extortion.

Why have such rights, in some legal systems, been extended beyond the fifty year period that already seemed sufficiently long? Is there a danger that human creativity will be diminished if copyright is restricted to a maximum of fifty years? Of course not. Extension of copyright has made life complicated for artists and scholars, and is of advantage only to a small group of corporations that have an interest in retaining a monopoly on certain creations not necessarily of their own invention. What was once a great step forward in the protection of the lonely and vulnerable artist has been turned into a means to protect economic interests that have already realized a profit. At a certain moment, we should insist, art must be free. The dialogue between the living and the dead must be allowed to proceed without restriction. Donald Duck and his relatives ought to belong not to a corporation but to the public domain, just as do Achilles and Agamemnon, Hector, Paris and Helen. Copyright should not be used to hinder the exchange of ideas or images.

It is extremely important that the relationship between copyright and creativity, between lawyers and artists, is held up to constant scrutiny. It is an honour if someone finds that what you have made or written is worthy of quoting. While that person should be free to quote, he should not be free to copy your work in such a way that he derives either honour or profit that belongs to you. It is important to maintain the right balance between what is mine and what is yours. And still, in due time, every creation should be allowed unhindered to find its way into that stream of creativity that is the basis of the human spirit.

Pierre Menard is the protagonist of a celebrated fiction by Jorge Luis Borges. So much did Menard admire *Don Quixote* that in the twentieth century he tried to create a new version: this turned out to be identical to the text of Cervantes. Menard's text is, according to Borges, even better than the 'original'. The story is enormously rich in its implications, though we can be fairly certain that it was not intended to stimulate reflection on copyright. The story is about the endlessly different ways of reading and understanding texts: it is about the processes of creativity and 'inspiration'. Copyright should not be a burden but a stimulus. We should be careful not to trap Pierre Menard, or a less extreme 'imitator', in a net spun by legal and economic interests purely for financial advantage. The creative struggle between past and present would then produce no works of art but only more and more of those documents that issue from court-rooms.

Further Reading

Adorno, Theodor W. and Max Horkheimer, *Dialectic of Enlightenment*, trans. John Cumming (London: Verso, 1979).

Andreotti, Libero, 'Play-tactics of the Internationale Situationniste', in OCTOBER 91, Winter 2000, pp. 37-58.

Aristotle, "Poetics", in *Classical Literary Criticism*, ed. D.A. Russell and M. Winterbottom (Oxford: Oxford University Press, 1972).

Baudelaire, Charles, 'Photography', in Beaumont Newhall (ed.), *Photography: Essays and Images* (New York: MOMA, 1980), pp. 112-113.

Barron, Anne, 'Copyright Law and the Claims of Art', (2002) *Intellectual Property Quarterly*. No. 4, pp. 368-401.

Barron, Anne, 'No Other Law? Author-ity, Property and Aboriginal Art', in Lionel Bently and Spyros Maniatis (eds.), *Intellectual Property and Ethics: Perspectives on Intellectual Property Vol. 4* (London Sweet & Maxwell, 1998), pp. 39-87.

Barron, Anne. "Copyright, Art and Objecthood". In *Dear Images. Art, Copyright and Culture*, edited by Daniel McClean and Karsten Schubert, 277-306. (London: Ridinghouse ICA, 2002).

Bentley, Lionel. "Art and the Making of Modern Copyright Law". In *Dear Images. Art, Copyright and Culture*, edited by Daniel McClean and Karsten Schubert, 331-351. (London: Ridinghouse ICA, 2002).

Benjamin, Walter, 'Kleine Geschichte der Photographie', in Walter Benjamin, *Gesammelte Schriften II, 1* (Frankfurt am Main: Suhrkamp Verlag, 1977), pp. 368-385.

Bernstein, Jay, *The Fate of Art: Aesthetic Alienation from Kant to Derrida and Adorno* (London: Polity Press, 1993).

Booton, David L. "Art in the Law of Copyright: Legal Determinations of Artistic Merit under United Kingdom Copyright Law". *Art, Antiquity and Law* 1, no. 2 (1996): 125-139.

Carroll, David, 'Community After Devastation' in Mark Poster (ed.), *Politics, Theory, and Contemporary Culture*, (New York: Columbia University Press, 1993), pp. 159-196.

Chartier, Roger. *The Order of Books. Readers, Authors, and Libraries in Europe between the Fourteenth and Eighteenth Centuries.* Translated by Cochrane, Lydia G. (Stanford: Stanford University Press, 1994).

Condorcet, Marie-Jean-Antoine Caritat Marquis de, "Fragments sur la liberté de la presse (1776)", in *Œuvres de Condorcet*, ed. M.-F. Arago (Paris: Didot, 1847), 253-314

Coombe, Rosemary, *The Cultural Life of Intellectual Properties: Authorship, Appropriation, and the Law* (London: Duke University Press, 1998).

Crary, Jonathan, *Techniques of the Observer: On vision and modernity in the nineteenth century* (Cambridge: The MIT Press, 1990).

Davies, Gillian. *Copyright and The Public Interest.* (Munich: Max Planck Institute for Foreign and International Patent, Copyright and Competition Law, 1994).

Deazley, Ronan. *On the Origin of the Right to Copy. Charting the Movement of Copyright Law in Eighteenth-Century Britain (1695-1775).* (Oxford: Hart Publishing, 2004).

Debord, Guy, *Report of the Construction of Situations and on the International Situationist Tendency's Conditions of Organisation and Action,*
at (http://www.slip,net/^knabb/S/report.htm).

Debord, Guy and Gil Wolman, A User's Guide to Détournement, *at (http:www.slip.net/^knabb/SI/detourn.htm).*

Douzinas, Costas and Lynda Nead (eds.), *Law and the Image: The Authority of Art and the Aesthetics of Law* (Chicago: The University of Chicago Press,1999).

Douzinas, Costas, Peter Goodrich and Yifat Hachamovitch, *Politics, Postmodernity, and Critical Legal Studies: The Legality of the Contingent* (London: Routledge, 1994).

Eagleton, Terry, *The Ideology of the Aesthetic* (Oxford: Blackwell, 2001).

Edelman, Bernard, *Le Droit saisi par la photographie – Éléments pour une théorie marxiste du droit* (Paris: Flammarion, 2001 [1973]).

Edelman, Bernard. "Création et banalité". *Recueil Dalloz Sirey*, no. Chronique (1983): 73-77.

Edwards, Elisabeth, *Imaginary Homecoming: Photography of Jorma Puranen* (Helsinki: Kustannus Pohjoinen, 1999).

Foster, Hal, *The Return of the Real* (Massachusetts: MIT Press, 2001).

Frizot, Michel, *The New History of Photography* (Köln: Köneman, 1998).

Gendreau, Ysolde, Axel Nordemann and Rainer Oesch (eds.), *Copyright and Photographs: An International Survey* (London: Kluwer Law, 1999).

Gernsheim, Helmut and Alison, *L.J.M Daguerre: The History of the Diorama and the Daguerrotype* (New York: Dower Publications, 1968).

Hansen, Miriam, 'Mass Culture as Hieroglyphic Writing: Adorno, Derrida, Kracauer', in Nigel Gibson and Andrew Rubin, *Adorno: A Critical Reader* (Oxford: Blackwell, 2002), pp. 57-85.

Hepp, François. "Le droit d'auteur "propriété incorporelle"?" *RIDA* XIX, no. Avril (1958): 161-191

Home, Stewart, *Neoism, Plagiarism & Praxis* (Edinburgh: AK Press, 1995).

Home, Stewart, *The Assault of Culture: Utopian Currents from Lettrisme to Class War* (Edinburgh: AK Press, 1991).

Hughes, Justin, "The Philosophy of Intellectual Property," *Georgetown Law Journal* 77, no. 2 (1988): 287-366. Simon Stokes, Art and Copyright. 2 ed. (Oxford: Hart Publishing, 2003 (2001))

Jay, Martin, 'Must Justice Be Blind?', in Costas Douzinas and Lynda Nead (eds.), *Law and the Image: The Authority of Art and the Aesthetics of Law*, pp. 19-35.

Jaszi, Peter, 'Toward a Theory of Copyright: The Metamorphoses of 'Authorship', (1991) Duke L.J. 455.

Jaszi, Peter, 'On the Author Effect: Contemporary Copyright and Collective Creativity', in Martha Woodmansee and Peter Jaszi (eds.), *The Construction of Authorship: Textual Appropriation in Law and Literature* (London: Duke University Press, 1994), pp. 29-56.

Jorn, Asger, Détournement as Negation and Prelude, *at (http://WWW.slip.net/^knabb/SI/3.detour.htm).*

Julius, Anthony, 'Art Crimes', in Daniel McClean and Karsten Schubert (eds.) *Dear Images: Art, Copyright and Culture* (London: Ridinghouse/ICA, 2002), pp. 473-503.

Kant, Immanuel, 'On the Wrongfulness of Unauthorised Publication of Books', in Mary J. Gregor (ed.) *Kant's Practical Philosophy* (Cambridge: Cambridge University Press, 1998), pp.29-35.

Kaplan, Benjamin. *An Unhurried View of Copyright*. (New York: Columbia University Press, 1967).

Karnell, Gunnar W.G. "The Idea/Expression Dichotomy – A Conceptual Fallacy". *Copyright World*, no. 7 (1989): 16-17.

Kase, Francis J., *Copyright Thought in Continental Europe: Its Development, Legal Theories and Philosophy. A Selected and Annotated Bibliography*. (South Hackensack, NJ: Fred B. Rothman & Co, 1967)

Paul Kearns, *The Legal Concept of Art* (Oxford: Hart Publishing, 1998)

Krauss, Rosalind, *The Originality of the Avant-Garde and Other Modernist Myths* (Cambridge, Mass.: MIT Press, 1985).

Laclau, Ernesto, *Emancipation(s)* (London: Verso, 1994); Chantal Mouffe, *The Return of the Political* (London: Verso, 1993).

Laclau, Ernesto and Chantal Mouffe, *Hegenomy and Socialist Strategy: Towards a Radical Democratic Politics* (London: Verso, 1985).

Lacan, Jacques, *The Four Fundamental Concepts of Psychoanalysis*, ed. Jacques-Alain Miller, trans. Alain Sheridan (New York: W.W. Norton & Company, 1978).

Laddie, J. "Copyright: Over-strength, Over-regulated, Over-rated?" *European Intellectual PropertyReview* 5 (1996): 253-260.

Larochelle, Gilbert, 'From Kant to Foucault: What Remains of the Author in Postmodernism', in Lise Buranen and Alice M. Roy (eds.), *Perspectives of Plagiarism and Intellectual Property in a Postmodern World* (New York: SUNY Press, 1999), pp. 121-130.

Locke, John, *The Second Treatise of Civil Government and A Letter Concerning Toleration. Edited by J.W. Gough*, ed. C.H. Wilson and R.B. McCallum (Oxford: Basil Blackwell, 1948 (1690)).

Loewenstein, Joseph. *The Author's Due: Printing and the Prehistory of Copyright*. (Chicago: The University of Chicago Press, 2002).

Lutticken, Sven, 'The Art of Theft', *New Left Review* 13, Jan/Feb 2002, pp. 89-104.

Lury, Celia. Cultural Rights. Technology, Legality and Personality. Edited by John Urry, International Library of Sociology. (London: Routledge, 1993).

Macfarlanc, Alan. "The Mystery of Property". In *Property Relations: Sharing, Exclusion, Legitimacy*, edited by C. Hann. Cambridge: Cambridge University Press, 1998.

MacPherson, C.B., *The Political Theory of Possesive Individualism. Hobbes to Locke* (London, Oxford, New York: Oxford University Press, 1962).

McClean, Daniel, and Karsten Schubert, eds. *Dear Images: Art, Copyright and Culture*. (London: Institute of Contemporary Art and Ridinghouse, 2002)
.

Millinger, Donald M. "Copyright and the Fine Artist". *The George Washington Law Review* 48, no. 3 (1980): 354-376.

Maffesoli, Michel, *Maailman Mieli – Yhteisöllisen tyylin muodoista* (La Contemplation du Monde – Figures du style communautaire), trans. Mika Määttänen (Tampere: Gaudeamus, 1995).

Marchart, Oliver, 'Enacting the Unrealized: Political Theory and the Role of "Radical Democratic Activism"', in Okwui Enwezor et al (eds.), *Dokumenta 11_Platform1 Democracy Unrealized* (Kassel: Hatje Cantz, 2003), pp. 253-266.

Margolis, Joseph, *Interpretation: Radical but not Unruly: The New Puzzle of Art and History* (Berkeley: University of California Press, 1995).

Mauss, Marcel, *The Gift: The form and reason for exchange in archaic societies*, trans. W.D. Halls (London: Routledge, 1990).

Nancy, Jean-Luc, *The Inoperative Community*, trans. Peter Connor (Minneapolis: University of Minnesota Press, 1991).

Patterson, Lyman Ray. *Copyright in Historical Perspective*. Nashville: Vanderbilt University Press, 1968.

Patterson, Lyman Ray, "Copyright and the Public Interest", in *Copyright. Current Viewpoints on History, Laws, Legislation*, ed. A. Kent and H. Lancour (New York: R. R. Bowker Company, 1972), 43-49.

Plato, "The Republic", in *Classical Literary Criticism*, ed. D.A. Russell and M. Winterbottom (Oxford: Oxford University Press, 1972).

Rose, Mark. *Authors and Owners. The Invention of Copyright*. Cambridge MA: Harvard University Press, 1993.

Rotstein, Robert H. "Beyond Metaphor: Copyright Infringement and the Fiction of the Work". *Chicago-Kent Law Review* 68, no. 2 (1993): 725-804.

Saunders, David, *Authorship and Copyright* (London: Routledge, 1992).

Schrift, Alain D. (ed.), *The Logic of The Gift: Toward an Ethic of Generosity* (London: Routledge, 1997).

Sherman, Brad, and Lionel Bentley. *The Making of Modern intellectual Property Law. The British Experience, 1760-1911*. (Cambridge: Cambridge University Press, 1999).

Smiers, Joost. *Art under Pressure: Promoting Cultural Diversity in the Age of Globalization*. (London, New York: Zed Books, 2003).

Solomon-Godeau, Abigail, *Photography at the Dock: Essays on Photographic History, Institutions, and Practices* (Minnesota: Minnesota University Press, 1991).

Stokes, Simon. *Art and Copyright*. (Oxford: Hart Publishing, 2003 (2001))

Tagg, John, *The Burden of Representation: essays of photographies and histories* (Basingstoke: Macmillan, 1988).

Tamm, Ditlev, *Roman Law and European Legal History* (Copenhagen: DJØF Publishing, 1997)

Walravens, Nadia, 'La Notion d'Originalité et Les Oeuvres d'Art Contemporaines', *Revue Internationale du Droit d'Auteur* (RIDA) 181 (1991), pp. 96-165.

Watson, Ben, *The Theory of Value in Marx and Adorno*, a presentation at 'Marxism and the Visual Arts Now: An International Conference', 8 April 2002, University College London.

Watt, Richard. *Copyright and Economic Theory. Friends or Foes?* (Cheltenham, UK: Edward Elgar, 2000).

Woodmansee, Martha. *Author, Art, and the Market. Rereading the History of Aesthetics*. (New York: Columbia University Press, 1996).

Woodmansee, Martha, and Peter Jaszi, eds. *The Construction of Authorship. Textual Appropriation in Law and Literature*. (Durham NC: Duke University Press, 1994).